Transparencies

"I like these poems a lot . . . They are clear and refreshing."
-- John Ashbery

"These are poems that touch the heart - a journeyer on the west coast looking back to her origins on the east coast: growing up, first love, vocation, death, elegies for loved ones lost. They offer continuing points of contact with the divine - a world redeemed through poetry."
-- Paul Mariani

"My main impression is that the poems are pools of articulate reflection: still surfaces with inner depths, or mirroring an outer world in the world within -- unless it is the inward discovering itself in the apparently outward. What seem to me the richest and strongest poems all have this doubling quality. It involves an effect of transparency, or translucency -- a seeing through the mirror, and a showing through."
-- David Moody

ALSO BY CAROLYN GRASSI

Poetry

JOURNEY TO CHARTRES
(Black Swan Books) 1989

Religion

MARY MAGDALEN AND THE WOMEN IN JESUS' LIFE
(Sheed and Ward) 1986
(co-authored with Joseph Grassi)

CAROLYN GRASSI

POEMS

TRANSPARENCIES

✳

for dear Peggy,
Thank you for your
loving presence
Blessings always,
Carolyn
July 21, 2005

First Edition

© 2003 by Carolyn Grassi

Published by Patmos Press
San Francisco, California

Available from: Small Press Distribution
1341 Seventh Street
Berkeley, CA 94710-1409

(800) 869-7553
E-mail: orders@spdbooks.org
www.spdbooks.org

Cover design by Judy July of Generic Type
Cover photo: Point Reyes, California by Carolyn Grassi

ISBN 0-9742435-0-7

In memory of my father Edwin A. Cook
and grandmother Florence Skea Ball

I am ever grateful to the late James Merrill for his friendship and generous Ingram Merrill Foundation Grant Award and to the late Harry Ford of Knopf who nominated this collection for a Pushcart Prize. My thanks to friends in the arts who read these poems and offered encouragement-- Ivan Argüelles, Jack Foley, Walter Martin, Diane Dreher, Diane Middlebrook, James Torrens S.J., Robert Hass, Galway Kinnel, Louis L. Martz, Ron Hansen, Calder Lowe, Penelope Dinsmore, Marguerite Fletcher, Mary Heffron, the late Naomi Clark and John Walsh. I wish to gratefully acknowledge David Moody for invaluable editorial advice.

Warm thanks to friends who shared the journey--Liz Carr, Carol Connolly, Mary Carr, Thérèse Gagnon, Marita and Jerry Grudzen, John Hawley, Julie Heath, Kristen Khoobyarian, Phyllis Koestenbaum, Judy Hanley Mauro, Joanne and John Landers, Delia McGrath, Helen McStravick, Ilse and Daniel Meyer, Betty and Peter Michelozzi, Mary O'Connor, Mary Jeanne Oliva, Ann Paras, Helen Prochaska, Bettina Rosenbladt, Barbara Rothchild, Jo-Ann and Jack Seiquist, Fred Tollini S.J., Cat Urbas and Raj Mohabir, Maria Vittoria West, Tennant C. Wright S.J., the late Ralph Brown, Elaine Lysne, Ted Mackin S.J. and Pauline Thompson. Sincere thanks to friends in the healing arts-- Catherine Duckgeischel, Joseph Henderson, Efrem Korngold, John Lee and Neil Russack.

Abiding gratitude to my mother Betty (Ball) Cook, brothers Richard and John Cook and their families. And for sharing the adventure of literature, I thank my writer sons Eddie and Peter, plus daughters-in-law Alisa and Maria. Deep thanks to my husband Joseph for his listening heart, sage advice and encouraging words.

Poems published from
Transparencies

"Ordinary Sundays"
"Celibacy"
"Sunrise, East Windham, New York"
"Westchester, New York"
"Renoir's Obsession"
"Finding You in San Francisco, Mark Rothko"
"Paula and Rilke"
"Your Letter"
"The Whiteness of Franz Marc"
"My Animus Fox, Franz Marc"
"Orpheus and Euridice"
"Ancestors"
"Annunciation"
"Sanctuary"
"After A Seven Year Drought"
"Natural Bridges, Santa Cruz"
"The Almond Tree, San Jose, California"
"Mendocino Headlands, Whale Watching"
"Photography"
"New Camaldoli Hermitage, Big Sur"
"Christ at Hand"
"Flying Home From Hoboken, New Jersey"
"Chagall's Window, Strasbourg"
"To Lose"

Grateful acknowledgement is made to the editors of
the following journals where these poems first appeared:

*Santa Clara Review, Negative Capability, Cesura,
(San Jose Center for Poetry), Rhino,Passages North,
Psychological Perspectives, Italian Americana, Oyez
Review, The Monserrat Review, America Magazine*

CONTENTS

Foreword

At one time a member of a Catholic Religious Community (Maryknoll), Carolyn Grassi's attendant vision flares from Dante to Flatbush, or in any direction the heart's questioning will take it, mysterious inter- and re-actions to life as experienced once and for all, tenderly and at times in a sort of bewilderment: what is to be "known", or understood" is not necessarily graspable. Rather it is preferable not to apprehend the "summum bonum", the thing that is transfigured, however transparent it may appear to be.

"Asalaam aleikum," and your body's shivering
when the chi descended at your son's birth,
like the pulse in a Beethoven sonata.

While the poems in TRANSPARENCIES, ordered in the rotational frame of Ms Grassi's peregrinations, have the immediacy of what passes for "confessional" literature, insofar as the autobiographical element is salient and the fulcrum from which the soul "takes off", they transcend the definition and assume an interior depth one associates with the poetry of Pound or H.D. As we move from East Coast, to various evocations of other geographies, and settle into the West Coast, a gradual transformation has taken place, including long meditations on the painterly, not unlike such excursions by Frank O'Hara. We are reminded by these poems that the mythical is never far off, that mingled with natural forms, the shapes of the "divine" hover in an air above us as we move from predawn shadows into the light: " . . . a triple-tiered fountain lifting the darkness into light as Orpheus calls Eurydice again and again . . . "

i

In an era dominated by the machine and its overlooked transgressions, to encounter such really "catholic poetry", imbued with an almost medieval sincerity, is the rarest thing. We do believe with the poet that Christ is at hand:

A small mirror, rented at the entrance
draws Christ from the ceiling into my hands.

Transfiguration or Ascension?

This magnificent man swimming among angels . . .

In these representations we are reminded of such early masters as Giotto or Cimabue, and we are indeed transported to that "other" world, a sense of stucco and humidity, dew and drenching sunlight, aspirations to move among the unmoved below the mountains that introduce us ultimately to the Pacific Ocean somewhere near Santa Cruz, California. And it is precisely the "local" within the cosmos that magnifies Ms Grassi's poetic sensibilities, a landscape shared with Robinson Jeffers with more than a generous dappling of the celestial, and the enigmatic "faith" that underscores it.

- Ivan Argüelles

I

Who knows the individual hour in which
. . . habits were first sown even as a seed?

- William Wordsworth

New York had all the iridescence
of the beginning of the world.

- F. Scott Fitzgerald

ORKNEY ANCESTORS

A blustery Autumn afternoon. The sun
due south wavers across the horizon.
Faint moments of lingering light

before clocks are turned back.
By four the day will begin to leave,
all dark by six. Mists reminding

me of grandma, born and raised
in this climate. Always hungering
for summer on the darkest days

of a Brooklyn winter. I knew
our people emigrated to Aberdeen
off the Orkneys. Ancestors perhaps

set tall stones in a circle
to lure the dawn. A far cry
from my brothers and me in Flatbush

as we ran to the lamp-post at dusk
in July or August. The rituals of games
lasting till dark. Orkney omens

whispered by relatives on holidays.
"Don't tell others about Aunt Nancy's
webbed toes." Her weary-eyed mother

searching the North Sea for her father's
ship. Worry was taking its toll.
Six children and another on the way.

Brooklyn, a supposed haven, yet always
this longing for Scotland. Grandma
sitting for hours under the maples lining

Prospect Park where the last light
filtered past her Second Street rooms
before it torched the Statue of Liberty.

SAINT MACHAR'S, OLD ABERDEEN

On the east side of Saint Machar's
cold North Sea winds tear at the elms.
Tombstones say Skye, not Skea.

Grandma sang hymns here as a girl.
Today the minister sprinkles
his sermon with lively phrases

unlike the homilies I heard in Brooklyn.
"How poor we'd be without the delectableness
of rogues. We all ought to embrace

the outsiders, whether Moslem or Roman
Catholic." A tea and biscuit reception
follows afterwards in the vestibule.

Everyone wants a word with the new pastor.
I remember grandma became a Catholic
at Uncle Howard's urging.

She missed the minister shaking her hand
after the service. Our Brooklyn parishes
were too crowded for such hand-shaking.

Uncle Howard owned the home rented by
grandma and grandpa. He insisted the children go
to Catholic schools. He spent his spare time

reading Aquinas' *Summa Theologica*.
Grandma kept quiet about Aunt Nancy's
two webbed toes, till Richie announced

his wedding plans, so she told his fiancee
Loretta about our family secret.
A Rossetti woman with dark hair holds

a rose in the Aberdeen art gallery.
She resembles grandma. Our people emigrated
to the mainland from the North Sea Orkneys.

Grandma insisted we walk round ladders,
knock on wood, notice the wind calling.
Only enough time to drive past Loch Ness.

THE MAROON BIKE

i.

Our landlord, Mr. Slattery's forbidden
barbed-wire fence guarded untended roses

we plucked if he wasn't watching. For my tenth
December birthday Dad drove me to his old

Gowanis Canal neighborhood, to Mike's Used Bikes
on Hamilton Avenue. Love at first sight--

a 2nd hand maroon bike, white striped fenders,
silver handle bars, thick nearly-new tires.

For months I saved candy money, wanting
maroon and white streamers and a shiny

silver bell. I simonized every inch.
This was freedom and adventure--

peddling as fast as I could to the other side
of Flatbush, those tree-lined streets,

two-storey homes, wide porches, lush lawns
where Mom lived as a girl on East Second,

a home owned by grandpa's brother,
Uncle Howard who insisted she attend

Catholic school, hoping all the family
would convert, so undo the deed

his father did in running off
with his wife's best friend. He saved

every penny for the church, as he had
for his mother when she was alive.

Riding the Flatbush Bus to St. Joseph's
High School on Willoughby and Jay Street

I'd see snow falling on Uncle Howard's
bare head. No overcoat, he was saving

the 25 cent fare. His will stipulated
over $200,000 to Catholic Charities

and the Society for the Propagation
of the Faith, $1,000 to Mom who always

invited him for Thanksgiving and Christmas,
visited him regularly in the hospital

and attended to his financial matters,
$500 to his widowed sister-in-law,

grandma, who lived in a third floor walk-up,
two rooms I'd visit after riding my bike

through Prospect Park on Saturdays,
calling loudly by her front stairs--

"Grandma! Grandma!" since she had no phone,
doorbell or elevator. Her daughter, my Mom,

now 88, hasn't been back east for fifteen years.
Will I buy a ten-speed and ride the coast.

ii.

An avid Brooklyn Dodger fan I exchanged
ten Elsie Borden Ice-cream wrappers

for a free pass to a Saturday game.
In pre-season my brother John and I rode

our bikes along Bedford Avenue
to Ebbets Field. We'd pry open a grey

corrugated gate, shimmy it loose
for a two foot crawl space to slip under.

In the empty stadium we worked our way
down the base line heading for Home Plate.

We offered the players lemonade
till a security guard told us to leave.

That summer before high school
I pursued the team, finally getting

each player's autograph on the beat-up baseball
I pinched during their practice games,

guys I and my friends adored-- Pee Wee Reese,
Duke Snyder, Johnny Podres, Sandy Kofax,

Jackie Robinson, Junior Gillian, Carl Furillo,
Roy Campanella and my favorite Gil Hodges

whom I tried to follow home, chasing
his car till my bike bumped his fender

at the intersection of Eastern Parkway
and Rogers Avenue. Years later my sister-in-law

Loretta surprised me, saying she saw Gil Hodges
almost every Sunday at Saint Vincent Ferrer

Parish's 10 o'clock Mass. News I heard
too late being as I was in the convent.

No bicycles. No T.V. No baseball scores.
Besides by then the team had left for L.A.

Come Spring, I sport a grey T-shirt with dark blue
lettering across my heart, *Brooklyn Dodgers*.

ORDINARY SUNDAYS

for Robert Hass

You thought it was ordinary-- everyone believing
in the soul especially at Easter when you wore
a blue coat trimmed by white, while John and Richie

fidgeted beside you as the priest lit the huge
candle, intoning the "Alleluia," so you jumped
to your feet answering "Amen! Amen!"

year after year at Holy Cross Parish
on the corner of Church Avenue and Veronica Place
three blocks east of Flatbush Avenue,

in what was called "the heart of Brooklyn."
And out west in Bob's class at San Jose State
a student laughed at your using the word "soul"

in a poem. Her saying-- "Why use such a word
when no one believes in it anymore." And you
stayed silent, embarrassed by having been

in the convent. Afterwards Bob suggested
that you read *"The Poetry of Meditation"*
by Louis Martz around the time you found

Bettleheim's book claiming Freud was
translated wrongly in America-- "Psyche
meant soul, not the mind." And hadn't

Aquinas spent his life trying to prove the soul's
existence; its stunning presence acknowledged
by Buddhists like Koben Chino who bowed

to everyone at the Los Altos Zendo and such
a sheen on the pink and white plum petals
by your San Jose window at Easter,

the whirl of white sleeves as you and Joe were
dancing with the Sufis in the Santa Cruz mountains
at the Unitarian Church on Freedom Boulevard--

"Asalaam aleikum," and your body's shivering
when the chi descended at your son's birth,
like the pulse in a Beethoven sonata.

OWL'S HEAD PARK, BROOKLYN

Warm sea air scenting our rented railroad
rooms as the day lingers into twilight
across Flatbush Avenue. We drive past
Greenwood Cemetery where great-grandpa
Captain George Skea and great-grandma Alice
are buried. At the turn of the century
they traveled by train from Aberdeen to Liverpool,

setting sail for Brooklyn with their children--
Al, Nancy, Florence, Harry, Ethel and Sidney.
We ride through the rough Gowanis Canal streets
of Dad's childhood, past the Brooklyn Navy yard
where Aunt Muriel works as a secretary
to Bay Ridge, Hamilton Parkway's
tree-lined streets, brick homes with gardens,
where Mom and Dad stroll hand in hand along the pier
as Richie, John and me run for the ropes thrown
by sailors to tie up their ships. Then grandma
and grandpa buy us a Good Humor pop--
Richie's pistachio, John's vanilla, mine's coconut.
Chasing each other, we kids climb Owl's Head Park's
highest hill up the tall maple overlooking the harbor--
buoys, tug boats, freighters, luxury liners,
New Jersey high-risers, misty Staten Island,
glowing Manhattan skyscrapers and the state-rooms
of a luxury liner's circle of lights rippling on the water
where the Hudson widens below the George Washington
Bridge and the Palisades' burnt-siena cliffs opposite
The Cloisters' foresty wall near the edge of the Bronx.

JACOB RIIS PARK BEACH, BROOKLYN

Waves forming past where we can see,
undertow pulling, high tide approaching,
Richie dives into crest after crest,
I follow, jumping up and down, springing
off the ocean floor till I can't touch bottom,
treading water I am tossed upside down,
bubbles hissing in my ears, sandy white foam
stinging my eyes, blond shafts of light
in the green darkness then I am washed
by a huge wave towards the burning sand,
the worn pink blanket and faded blue umbrella
as I turn to see Richie swimming past the jetty.

BASH-BISH FALLS, TACONIC STATE PARK, N. Y.

Our only family vacation up-state New York,
Taconic State Park near the Massachusetts border.
We find a general store for the first time,
fascinated by the jam jars, food bins,
bolts of fabric, pen knives and bales of hay.
A week in a white cottage with its banging
screen door. Two weather-worn rocking chairs
on the wide porch. Richie, waving a snake,
chases John and me across the lawn. We ride
our bikes to Bash-Bish Falls. Jump into
its icy pool, floating under puffy clouds
and quaking aspen. Kicking and splashing
to keep warm. We fill our cheeks with water,
spit sprays overhead. Richie leaps under
the falls. John and I dog-paddle towards shore.
Three of us stretch across the hot boulders.
Steam rises between our fingers. We pretend
to live over the ridge. In six years I'll enter
the convent overlooking the Hudson River.

CAMP OH-NEW-TAH, EAST WINDHAM, N. Y.

The IRT Flatbush Line to Grand Central Station,
 then the cross-town shuttle. We're walking west
 towards Tenth Avenue and 49th Street.
Damp asphalt, dark alleys, garbage cans, buses,
cars, taxis, trucks. Dad holds my ten year old
hand. We reach the store front Herald Tribune's
Fresh Air Camp Center in the heart of Hell's Kitchen.
I wait on the hard bench till my name's called.
Boarding the bus, I turn round to wave goodbye
to Dad who sets off for his work at Whitehead Brothers
(Mormon run) Company on West 32nd. The bus rumbles
through the Holland Tunnel. Yellow tiles whiz by.
Small glass booths housing guards like Dad's friend

Jimmy Dorian who works five days a week
watching the red lights blinking. We stop,
start, stop, start, rise towards the Jersey shore,
turn north for up state New York. I glance
at the sky-scrapers sparkling across the river.
Everyone's singing-- "I love to go a wandering
along the mountain track and when I go,
I love to sing, my knapsack on my back."
"Swing low sweet chariot . . ." "When I was
a camper at Oh-Neh-Tah, I lived by the side
of the lake, quack, quack . . ." Clapping,
humming, tossing lines back and forth.
Sweet spirituals. Swinging chariots.
The bus rocks past maples, hickories, elms,
birches, pines of the Palisades, the Ramapos,
Rip Van Winkle territory, East Windham
hazy Catskill Mountains overlooking
the huge valley view of three states--
New York, Connecticut and Massachusetts
not far from the sign saying-- "Oh-Neh-Tah."
Young women's voices rising from the forest
ringing Silver Lake-- "We welcome you to
Oh-Neh-Tah, we're mighty glad you're here.
We'll sing you in. We'll sing you out. To you
we'll raise a mighty shout. Hail, hail,
the gang's all here and you're welcome
to Oh-Neh-Tah." I'm eager and nervous, waiting
to hear who'll I live with for the next two weeks.

CAMPFIRE

Blue poster-paint completely covers my body,
Judy's green, Arlene's red, Barbara's yellow,

matching feathers in our hair, bells tickling
our ankles, we hop through ribbon hoops,

the drum beats-- toe . . . heel . . . toe . . . heel . . .
round and round the roaring campfire

till Miss Dot in full feathered head-dress
stretches her arms towards the night sky,

signaling for silence, her voice ringing
across the valley-- "Manitou, Great Spirit,

hear our call." Bowing to the north, south,
east and west, she puffs the peace pipe

then passes it round the circle of campers.
Miss Mary strikes the drum leading us

to jump through our rainbow hoops closer to
the flames-- toe . . . heel . . . toe . . . heel . . .

red, blue, green, yellow ribbons flying
past the circle of girls who wear woolen blankets

and the multicolored feathers of cabins named
Winnebago, Chippewa, Papago, Onedoga, Sebago,

Witchita, Shawnee, Kickapoo. Hum, humming, hum.
Sparkling fire, girls leaping under moon and stars.

SUNRISE, EAST WINDHAM, NEW YORK

I saw the sun rise for the first time
through a mountain pass when I was ten,
standing on a ledge at the top of Mount Zorn
facing Windham High Peak and Dane's Hill.
The fog was disappearing slowly
as the shining ball worked its way through
clouds, streaking a white path across the dark
blue and green hills, then suddenly we stopped

talking as the golden disc descended into Silver Lake
setting it afire and someone began singing--
"Silver Lake was named by the Indians,
named by the Indians many years ago."
This was why Miss Mary made us rise in the dark
to put on extra clothes so we city girls might see
the workings of morning on the pine cones,
maples, aspens, birches and elms, brightening
the fields, cabins, boat house and dining hall,
warming the dew in blue-bells and buttercups,
coating the swimming lagoon with plumed vapors.
There were bird calls and animals rustling in the forest
as we sang-- "Morning comes early and bright with dew,
under your window I sing to you. Up then
with singing, up then with singing. Let us be
greeting the morn so blue . . ." Such a thrill
for Judy, Barbara, Aileen, Penny, Gwen and me--
girls from Flatbush, Bensonhurst, Hell's Kitchen,
Red Hook, Canarsie, Grave's End, Sheepshead Bay,
East New York, the Lower East Side, Harlem,
the Bronx and Bay Ridge, ten year old girls
gathering twigs and fallen branches
to form an A-frame over three large logs,
till Miss Mary struck a wooden match
against a grey stone held in her palm,
setting the tinder aflame to cook oatmeal
in a heavy pot, warming our hands and legs
as the lemony light spread through the forest
while the bright ball of sun withdrew
into a corner of clouds high above the valley.

DAPHNE AND APOLLO IN BROOKLYN

In the Greek legend Apollo clings to Daphne's
branching figure. She ran. He pursued.

Was my desire like Apollo's, in grade school
dreaming up ways to win Jimmy Morris?

My letter sent from summer camp: "Can we dance?"
His obliging "once" on a Friday night in August.

A slow one in the boys' schoolyard with Elvis
under the stars. Then afternoons playing street-ball

outside his house on the other side of Flatbush.
Laughing loud so he'd hear me. Needing to see

him bound down the front porch under a canopy
of maples. Wanting him to turn round and wave.

Hoping he'd say "Hi." Praying he'd say "Yes"
and he did say "Yes" to my Junior Prom.

I danced hard as I could; he stayed rigid
in my arms even during the lindy.

Nothing made him relax, not Nat King Cole,
not Fats Domino, not Elvis, not Little Richard,

not the Platters. Then the subway ride home
in utter silence. A week later the shock

of seeing him hand in hand with Margaret Anderson
along Nostrand Avenue. I ducked in a doorway.

The last time we met he shouted in a crowd
as he passed me at the IRT Newkirk station--

"I hear you're entering the convent."
"They say you're becoming a priest."

"No. Never." I still see his deep blue
Irish eyes, his strong shoulders,

his dark curly hair. He won every
academic prize and attended Brooklyn Prep.

The legend says Daphne ran,
Apollo pursued. I entered the convent.

THE IMPERIAL DUKES

in memory of Aileen Cleary

All the rough stuff my brother Richie did
or did not do that Spring he sported a leather jacket,
a garrison belt, heavy boots and wore his hair
in a "d.a." Looking a lot like Elvis he turned up
ready for trouble on the other side of Flatbush
in what I thought was a "better neighborhood"
than ours, till those kids drew him into their ranks
and made it a teenage test of manhood to join in
"a rumble. " Aileen Cleary fell into a worse fate
since she didn't leave "The Tigresses" as Richie
left "The Imperial Dukes" after first joining.

The last time I met Aileen was accidentally
on a rainy Friday night along Nostrand Avenue.
She called to me-- "Hey! Cookie!" I didn't recognize her
behind the thick mascara, bright red lipstick,
pulled back hair, leather jacket, tight jeans
and sling back shoes. She looked terribly tough.
I thought her face was drenched by rain
till I heard her sobbing as she said--
"Billy dumped me and I don't know what to do.
I've gotta find him. See ya, Cookie."

My first year as a Maryknoll postulant I received
a letter from Joan Burke, a Holy Cross classmate,
"I know you'd want to know, since you and Aileen
were close. She died recently of a brain tumor."
She was the smartest, funniest, prettiest,
wildest girl I ever knew. We sat side by side
in class, Cook following Cleary. She sent notes
when the teacher's back was turned. She drew
cartoons, made faces, waved her arms and never
got caught, not even when Sister called on her
suddenly. She always knew the answer. I was less
lucky in hiding my mischief as I fumbled for answers.

One balmy Spring afternoon Aileen knocked
on our apartment door. "Come on. Let's explore
the neighborhood." We jumped over Mr. Knight's fence,
then shimmied up between two high walls to sit
on the edge of an old garage, our legs swinging
over an empty lot facing Bekins Warehouse.
She spoke in a low confidential tone--
"You know, Cookie, you can get 'it' anytime."
"Yeah. I know." (Pretending I knew).
"I mean like 'it' can happen now or
tomorrow. You just look and 'it's' there."
"Yeah." "Did you get 'it' yet?" "No."
"Did you?" "No. But I will soon. I just
know I will." "And it's easy to get
pregnant." "Yeah. I know what you mean."
Wishing and not wishing she would
tell me all the secrets she knew . . .

Almost everyone we knew in Brooklyn
moved to Long Island, Rockland County
or Jersey. Richie became a computer whiz,
married his high school sweetheart, Loretta,
raised six kids in Suffern County near
Bear Mountain. In the convent I fell
in love with Joe. We married secretly
at Saint Mark's rectory in Greenwich Village
under a poster of Che Guevera. We raised
our sons, Eddie and Peter, in San Jose, California.
My brother John never joined a gang, only the US
Navy during the Vietnam War. He married
his college sweetheart, Terry, and raised
their son in the Santa Cruz Mountains.
John became a San Jose Police Lieutenant,
his speciality with Santa Clara County schools--
how to prevent kids from joining gangs.

OUR FATHER

i.

Our father was young, handsome, indestructible
or so we thought at age six or seven
when he was thirty-three and taught us how
to glide over the Atlantic waves and we watched
him and his brother John far out past the breakers.
His arms arcing gracefully one by one, his steady kick,
his turning over, whale-like spitting water,
then swimming parallel to shore, heading for
the next beach, disappearing behind the jetty.

ii.

You picked me up at the convent. We were driving
down the Sawmill River Parkway when you said:
"I've got to pull over." Were you suddenly sick?
You began crying. We were on our way to
Holy Family Hospital in Brooklyn Heights,
the day after Dad's surgery for pancreatic cancer,
the next to last night of his life.

iii.

You became the kind of father he was.
I've watched you play with your six children
the same games Dad played with you, John and me.
Each kid runs towards you as you lie on the floor,
then you flip them over your legs, so they somersault
in air and land on their feet laughing. You swing Erin high,
steady her feet as she spreads her arms horizontal,
slowly you let go, so she stands alone on your shoulders.

iv.

Our northern California coast is too cold for swimming,
Too wild a surf. The day after we moved to San Jose,
Joe drove the boys and me over the Santa Cruz Mountains
to Natural Bridges State Beach. I dived into the icy suds
feeling the thrill of coming up into the light beyond
the breakers as I watched them roll ashore. Soon numb
I headed in. Now I only wade. You've never swum out west.
Each visit you insist on climbing down Seal Rock Cliff
for the cave where the ocean leaps wildly by your feet.

v.

You fly home east into that earlier time zone,
back to the familiar warm waters of Rockaway,
Jones's Beach, Sunken Meadow or Jacob Riis Park
in the borough of Brooklyn where Dad is buried
in Flatbush, twenty minutes from the Atlantic.

II

Mornings are mysteries;
the first world's youth . . .

- Henry Vaughan

The secret food of fires unseen,
could thou but be what thou hast been.

- Shelley

LEAVING HOME

At sixteen after announcing "my news"
Mom and Dad seemed complacent.
No "No." No "Why?" No pressure, only:
"What about the local nuns, why join
an Order that will send you so far away?"

I was entranced by the photo of a Maryknoll
Sister dressed in a white habit
using a pole to wade down the Beni River
in Bolivia, and stories of Theophane Venard
hiking through the rice paddies of China.

The world far from Brooklyn drew me--
exotic places, new languages,
and a voice rubbing my soul
towards sacrifice, besides the boy
I loved . . . loved someone else.

Recently Mom recalled the day
I entered, September 2nd. She, Dad
Richie and John waved goodbye
at the convent door. Driving home
they stopped at a Westchester diner,

where Dad broke down and cried.
Perhaps his dying six years later,
at age 51, created the crisis
I needed to question my vocation.
The following year I left the Order.

CELIBACY

I lie on the grass at Natural Bridges Park waiting for
your return from back east. It is one week since
we last made love. Earth's touch a reminder of that time
of voluntary celibacy, eighteen to twenty-five.

Years of vague longings in Massachusetts on the hill
facing west into the sunset. I leaned against the birches
as they caught the wind in their hair, whispering and bending
towards each other. Retreat days in all that silence . . .
I roamed the forest's edge and touched the ivy winding
round the pines. I stroked a moss bed, hiding a piece
of its yellow-green fur in my pocket. Wednesdays we hiked
to Ipswich Bird Sanctuary, where we ate lunch in a cave
overlooking the pond, then rested in a meadow, separate
yet near, hidden by high wild wheat, letting our dreams
become words that moved as clouds drifting over us.
Walking back to choir Miriam parted the ferns uncovering
a lady-slipper or spider's web. To each plant touched
by her hand she gave its proper name lingering in Latin.
At night in chapel we chanted Compline. "In manus tuas,
Domine, commendo Spiritum meum . . ." Incense encircled
the large beeswax candle lighting the face of someone
I strained sideways to see. Afterwards in the confessional
I listened to the man's deep melodious voice mix with
the scent of a neighbor's hearth. Later, with curtains pulled
back on my cubicle, the forest sounds entered.

THE NOVITIATE NEAR SALEM, MASSACHUSETTS

Hide and go seek was a game birds
played in the thickening maples,
aspens and birches that made

October glorious, though the days
were ending early at age twenty
as I leaned against a swaying birch

loving how the forest surrendered
to shade as the sun having
caressed each hairy pod and wild violet

24

ran down the ridge towards Salem.
Ferns were bending in the wind.
A lady-slipper swelled pale pink.

The underbrush glistened a gray-blue
with silky spidery traces
strung in damp, disappearing webs,

as I tried conjuring your face
through song and evening prayers
after a year's separation.

How distinct the fir needles
flickering and the shade inhaling
everything the day had given.

The maple sap hid in the sweet
tissued irises. Rock roses continued
to climb the cloister wall, tiny

pressure points, leafy cells on-call.
A neighbor's chimney smoldered.
Cloud banks gleamed above the rafters.

Hawks and owls were picking up
each other's echo. Yahweh became
a lover inhabiting the psalms.

A trio of birches acted as sentinels.
They swayed as the wind swooped
through their black and white figures.

CANONICAL YEAR, TOPSFIELD, MASSACHUSETTS

Silence blankets the open lawn. Embers of summer
glow in the scarlet forest. Off-shore breezes
evaporate quickly. My skin tingles in heavy serge.
Sister Miriam coaxes the sparrows. Tiny beaks bob

for the seeds she sprinkles with her whitened hand.
Twilight arrives a minute earlier than yesterday.
Poison ivy has grown thick and high in the pines.
My Theology teacher accuses me of being "superficial."
I ask Linda what it means? She says "Forget it."
Sister's wrong. You're being tested." Will I feel
physically changed on Profession Day, June 24th,
the feastday of John the Baptist, after vowing
Poverty, Chastity and Obedience before
Cardinal Cushing who will preside in scarlet robes.
Crocuses and Easter lilies come and go. Rock roses
scatter along the entrance road. I lift my arms,
palm touching palm, bow to my sisters in choir.
Maples brush the stained glass windows. Fire on fire.
October's almost extinguished. Jimmy married last
May. I wrap my woolen mantle close in the cool chapel.
Compline is intoned on the organ. Soon lights out.

IPSWICH BIRD SANCTUARY, MASSACHUSETTS

Birds in blue, orange, black and brown
offer songs amid high pitched calls.
Wild wheat tassels brush my arm.

This is a free Wednesday afternoon.
We hike to the Sanctuary after facing
three fierce collies who snap at our rosaries.

Clouds sit still in an expansive sky.
Five of us lie side by side talking
about the country we want as a mission.

We are all in our early twenties.
Ellen hopes she'll teach English in Japan,
Delore wants to be a doctor in Bolivia,

Beth a social worker in Africa,
I dream of working in the Marshall Islands.
Linda talks constantly about her family.

No one mentions men, except for priests.
A rock-cave refuge overlooks the pond.
Silence, bird calls, rustling bushes.

"Do you think Ann will be asked to leave,
since she hurt her back carrying those heavy
cleaning buckets?" "I want to ask

permission to talk in twos." We stop
on the way back under an old oak tree
half way down the front lawn

of a dilapidated estate we have
named "the ruins." Someone shouts--
"We'll be late for choir!"

Inside the chapel we pick up the edge
of our grey scapula, kiss it, bow,
then stretch one arm high overhead

as we kneel down, then slide sideways,
making the Venia towards the Tabernacle,
then one by one we file into our stall

on opposite aisles. Evelyn intones
the Psalms. Facing each other across
the nave we chant the Latin lines.

DIVINE OFFICE, TOPSFIELD, MASSACHUSETTS

Morning meditations, my mind wanders.
Snow blankets the inner courtyard.

Marianne says she is leaving. Sparrows bob
for holly berries. Scarlet tanagers

have vanished. Turn off the lamp, close
Aquinas' *Summa Theologica*. Am I ready

for a missionary assignment? My friends want
to go abroad; it's why we entered the Order.

Why do I consider the Cloister? Am I
called to be a contemplative? Am I afraid

of leaving America? Birches stiffen
in their thick white coats. The Hudson has

frozen all the way to Nyack. Forty miles
to the south Manhattan rises as a fantasy land,

misty skyscrapers glowing at sunset.
From the fourth floor Art Tower

Beth and I spot the Empire State Building.
After high school I worked as a secretary

at 121 East 39th off Park Avenue;
I often ordered swiss on rye with mustard

and a pickle for lunch around the corner
at the Lexington Avenue Deli. I miss

the city crowds. Community life can be
lonely. Eileen will stop in Portland

before boarding a freighter for the Philippines.
If I hide in the kitchen at night

I'll receive her call before she sails.
Yesterday we walked round Roger's forest.

During Compline, I studied the grace
in her bowing and wished I was like her.

A ten-year mission assignment sounds scary.
Am I a coward? Overly attached to Gregorian

Chant's deliciously sensual cadences,
the pulsating Psalms and formal genuflections.

Should I meditate more on Jeremiah's prophetic
call, Job's patience, Jesus' sacrifice.

If the divine exists everywhere, why not
return to Flatbush, Brooklyn, New York?

A WEEK AT WATCH HILL, RHODE ISLAND

This wide-porched beauty, thirty windows
overlooking the Sound. Women walking
side by side, rarely touching.

The passionate lines of the *Song of Songs*
chanted every season.
Late at night the moon brushing

across my bed. The lighthouse beam
flashing its distressful call.
Most ships docked, seagulls silent.

Muscles tense, my legs are restless,
nightgown sticky on my skin.
I suppress those places we're supposed to

ignore. Desire hides in Latin phrases
floating across the summer air
beyond dunes and a pine forest.

A July heat-wave tightens every hedge.
Prayer-beads slide through young fingers--
hands quieted, I study your gestures,

your eyes closed at Communion. Why are those
handsome men and vivacious women at ease
in the photo, circling the ship-shaped

dining room day in, day out.
Shall I slip a poem under your door?
We bow our heads horizontal

towards a purified loving,
"Sanctus, Sanctus, Sanctus,"
she and she and she dispersing divinity,

three bells in harmony across the Sound.
The buoy repeats its off shore call.
My footsteps muffled on the carpeted floor.

Humid rest periods. The phonograph playing
songs from the 60's downstairs in the parlor.
Women praying Prime, Terce, Sext, None . . .

Salty residue on my skin when I shower.
The weather-vane shifts. We stroll
back and forth overlooking the garden.

You keep speaking about our mission.
I'm completely distracted. The sun lingers
in the west. The Sound's a brilliant gold.

You avoid anything personal. Everything
must be filtered through grace, obligation,
universal love. I'm too embarrassed,

too self-conscious to speak affectionately.
We knead bread, shuck corn, peel forty
potatoes. Who's laughing inside the pantry?

We sip the chalice before breakfast.
Sunday afternoon's our final swim.
Reeds quiver by my waist, willows brush

your face, burning white sand underfoot,
nesting sea-birds and swelling green waves.
The fog-horn interferes with thoughts

of leaving. Rollers carry us. You turn
away. The sanctuary lamp's extinguished.
A yellow bus waits to take us inland.

DEPARTURE DAY, MARYKNOLL, NEW YORK

Our dorm window framed a neighbor's farm
shrouded in fog across the Hudson.
Scarlet maple leaves rubbed the birches

rimming Roger's pond where we ice-skated
that winter before your Japanese
assignment was announced in the refectory.

After lunch we climbed cloister-hill.
I was sad, tongue-tied, shy. You were
preoccupied with your new mission.

Our "custody of the eyes" rule
forbids direct glances into another's
face at "silent time." Looking at you

across the aisle at Vespers reminded me
of everything I longed to be. I first
noticed you chanting the Lamentations

of Jeremiah in choir. Clouds had covered
the sun, though your face was radiant.
Later I paced the cloister garden

gathering courage to write you a note.
You left at the end of October,
when the forest turns mauve and gold.

As the cab drove away I rang a New Year's Eve
noise-maker along with all the Sisters
celebrating your Departure to the Far East.

Bereft by the tabernacle, I hid my grief.
At night I scrubbed your cell floor--
soap suds, brillo pad, warm water, tears.

WESTCHESTER, NEW YORK

Through the apple boughs
I stare at the seminary pagoda,
considering love divine and undivine.

This cloistered mythic setting,
changing my name when I'm nineteen.
Poverty, Chastity, Obedience.

Retreat days in the wheat field,
a frill, not integral to our training,
unlike the novitiate's "real purpose"

gearing us towards foreign service.
I fear a ten year mission,
returning when those I love are being

sent away. How will I wave goodbye
to my family from the harbor?
Brooklyn is a poor solution.

At least not this immersion
in what some might call
"a light on the hill" complex

originating in Puritan New England,
though the founders of our Order
were Massachusetts Catholics.

I'm "free to leave," no one forced me
to join, I followed "a call,"
and love this place. Will I be

sent to Japan, Peru or Africa?
No one expresses worry.
We sing the psalms at night in choir.

House-lamps glow across the Hudson.
A meadowlark sways on a rain-soaked wire.
Stars shimmer over the Ramapos.

Intangible faith, why question
the givens? Will I ever go west?
At fourteen I idolized James Dean,

enjoyed basketball, dancing and swimming
at the beach, ignoring the fact that I was
becoming a woman. Only now do I notice

the convent is loosening its hold.
My superior is mistaken, thinking
I haven't found happiness here.

MY RELIGION

A New England path lined by fennel,
bull-rushes flanking the Sound.
No heavy cleaning for two weeks.

Relaxed in light grey cotton habits,
she surprised me--
"Your eyes are clear pools."

Embarrassed, I said nothing.
My Novice Mistress insisted:
"I can always tell what you are feeling,

even when you remain silent."
Later I misread "the signs,"
believing each wave pressed daring,

the wind courage,
the Holy Spirit meant
"Try again, don't give up!"

Slipping on a stone, I bled,
though failed to heed the warning--
God's white wafered body

dipped in his miraculous blood.
Wasn't suffering essential?
Sacramentality saturated everything.

If the sea swelled, if tides hesitated,
if a storm was sighted-- what were
their meanings? Marianne found

a sea-gull pierced by a sharp rock
along the shore. She worried about
her mother's recovery from surgery.

We were taught to stitch a pattern
together from each earthly gesture.
This became indelible. Years later

I misread the gift a man gave,
thinking the sea-pearl necklace
meant constancy, not farewell.

THE VIETNAM WAR

Whenever I pass by the sports field
at Brooklyn College, my Alma Mater,
the sense of that war returns.

There was a guy named Allen
who sat next to me in History class.
He wore a yarmulke. I tried hiding

the fact that I had left the convent
the year before. We used to chat
after Doctor Abbot's lecture.

Allen handed in a paper on the seeds of
anti-Semitism in Europe. Mine was on
the collapse of the League of Nations.

At term's end, side by side, we
struggled with the three-hour final
on events leading up to World War II.

After the exam we walked across
the sports field talking about
graduation in two weeks,

and his fear of the lottery,
since his number stood
at the top of the list.

"I don't think I'll be at
graduation." "Why?" "Because
I'm expecting a baby any day now."

"You're kidding!" "No. I really
mean it." He looked embarrassed,
maybe because he hadn't noticed

my pregnancy or was it a look of regret
at his own future fate decided by
gender and a lottery number.

AS LONG AS IT TAKES, BROOKLYN COLLEGE

By the Lily Pond studying "The New Left,"
wondering if I should become an activist
after my recent "release" from the convent.
Shy, uneasy on how to relate in the "world,"
I listen to handsome Doctor Berdenbrock
lecture on "surplus value."   Imagining Marx
bent over his desk in the British Library
or late at night in a poor section of London
hearing a woman cry at the news that her husband
has been fired. I'm beginning to wonder who
has the right to own the "means of production."
Should I volunteer for Bobby Kennedy's campaign,
Doctor Spock's Freedom and Peace Party
or the new Students for a Democratic Society
which sounds interesting. At the well-attended
SDS meeting a call goes out for students
to meet in small groups. I join ten other
girls in a Flatbush Avenue apartment
staging a plan to protest the war openly
in front of the synagogue on Saturday,
then "Meet on the green Wednesday at noon
before Boylan Hall to demonstrate against
the war and push for 'Open Admissions'
for Blacks and Hispanics. Be ready to occupy
the Administration for as long as it takes."

SISTER MARY XAVIER, M.M.

Named after the fiery Spanish missionary
"Francis Xavier," founder of the Jesuits,
yet the gentlest woman in a position
of authority within the Maryknoll Sisters.
Delicate, bent over by arthritis,
voice weakened by a heart-condition,
she in her seventies, I twenty-one
and newly arrived at our Motherhouse
after the rigors of Novitiate training,
having vowed Poverty, Chastity and Obedience.
Of that generation influenced by John XXIII
we were restless, rebellious about the Rule,
seeking "authenticity" and "personal growth,"
buzz words affecting our life-style, meaning
many would leave, including myself.
Years later and living in California I visited
"Xavier," as we called her, in Stockton.
Supposedly retired, she volunteered
at the local Social Work office asking
for a few cases considered hopeless.
So they assigned her a man who hadn't
cashed his Social Security check
for many years and turned away all
attempts at assistance. Several times she
knocked on his door to no avail,
finally pleading-- "Please let me have
a glass of water. I have a heart condition."
True enough and the temperature hovering
round 96 degrees. "Alright, but you better
leave right away and I don't want no
government help." She noticed a stack
of *National Geographic* on the table.
"Would you like some more?" "Maybe."
Thus their weekly visit began and
his Social Security check was reinstated.
And I had asked "are you doing anything now
that you're retired?" Memorable also

were her words when I was a novice,
homesick and confused. She held my hand
tightly as she looked intently at me
with her pale blue Irish eyes, saying
nothing, then slowly, strongly
the words-- "Sister, I believe in you."

III

All art is in someway a form of confession.

- James Baldwin

It is impossible to explain this to anyone
who is not to the same extent a follower
of Love; and to those who are it is obvious
what the meaning is.

- Dante

THE COTTAGE AT THE SHORE

Shallow salt water waves stain the pier
as we watch the sun disappear west.
Teasing and cajoling, you finger red highlights
in my dark hair. Your arm round my waist
you point out a white-porched beauty,
the home you once wanted.

Lush lawns separate each Hopper-like house.
A blue perpendicular sky trembling down the middle.
The sun fails to melt last night's icy pockets.
High tide sprays over the stone-wall
stinging my face. Doves nestle under eaves.
The tennis net's rolled up, locked in the shed.

Birches barely stir beside the pine grove.
Scarlet maples wave by the bedroom window.
Long Island's shimmering light across the Sound.
An optical illusion or trace-memory from childhood--
such a paradise Dad created in the summer
for a few days far from Flatbush,

the sparkling pebbles of Sunken Meadow State Beach
tickling our feet. At low tide Richie, John and I
hiked with Dad along sandbars. The horse-shoe
crabs were scary. We played tag on the hot sand.
Black groves cluster across the virginal expanse
of Long Island's outer ridge, Orient Point,

where Mom and Dad vacationed one summer
across from Watch Hill, Rhode Island. A final photo
shows him on the shore waving his baseball cap.
I saved his last letter about their fish dinner.
Nearby gulls disturb my concentration. I'm losing
those summer strands, losing the girl I was

and the woman I was becoming. Farewell to sea-facials,
kinky hair, salty skin, pine groves and birches,
tides leaping the stone wall, salt-water hidden
in roses, Long Island Sound where I swam
as a girl. I'm leaving, before being left,
having left another, will I be welcomed back?

The summer sailing lessons have ceased.
A few small boats zig-zag the cove. Soon they
flock towards the harbor. Young excited voices
pierced the air last July when I sailed
for the first time. My sailing-days are over.
Rushing through this picture-perfect town,

I pass the white-steeple church, red-brick town-
hall and gray-clapboard homes that keep
a lid on scandals overlooking "the green."
I slam the back door of my rented cottage,
roll the Hopper sailing poster into
its traveling container. Fly home fast.

THE COLLEGE COURTYARD

This medieval window frames the night.
I pull the drapes back while I watch

you cross the courtyard, silhouetted
by the lamp-post, till suddenly

you disappear into the dark.
Morning brings fresh footprints

crunchy in snow to dining hall,
classrooms, offices, dorms and library.

Each turret sparkles in its translucent
icy jacket. The pine branches have dipped

down with blankets of snow.
The bell tower pierces the clarity

of new found blue. Tear-like icicles
hang mid-way along the cloister.

Each gargoyle sticks out its
frozen tongue. The gate swings open

then closes. Teachers and students,
deans, secretaries and a few guests

come and go. There will be no knock
on the thick oak door like yours

last year after I heard your footsteps
on the slate steps, so rushed

breathless to meet you, feeling
the cold night air against your face.

THE FOREST

Cool gusty sprays hitting hard
as we sail past the Needle Islands.
The brilliant maples are fading

behind your back. The Sound suddenly
quiets. You toss off your news--
"I'll be leaving for the mid-west."

No pleading can alter your plans.
"Come on, don't get serious,
why spoil things by worrying.

Make do. Cheer up! That's a girl!"
After docking the boat I slip
on a pile of disintegrating leaves.

Summer has drained through
the forest's struggling core.
I leave a stone marred by lichen

by your door. Reversing my car,
I gaze at the elm branches
waving above your bedroom.

My pulse racing, I grip the wheel
as I hurry over the wooden-bridge
avoiding the rear-view mirror.

THE VILLAGE CAFE

Waiting by the window, close to the red
geraniums, I'm expecting him soon.

Biting cold December breezes. Townsfolk
bang the storm door. Most wear woolen scarves.

Squirrels skirt the green. Clouds gather.
The one I wait for will not change.

What is will leave its scar. Why carry things
further? Sweet currant scone and melting

butter, thick strawberry jam. Milk spots
swim in my dark French brew. I sip slowly.

Why not leave, since I'll be left.
The sun withers towards New York City.

I've become a Northern Californian.
Am now far from home. Geese have long gone.

Crimson leaves loosen. He's increasingly
secretive. Has he rehearsed his role?

I'm tired, embarrassed. Birch pods cling
in black cocoons. Frosty pine-needles crack.

Why fight fate? Avoid further hurt. Give in.
Give up. Say "No." Now go. The white church

on the square witnessed what happened--
leaning against the ancient oak I searched

the heavens for a sign. He desired tears
out in the open, also affection. Love

or grief must be demonstrative, no matter
the occasion. "Sorry, but loving two women

isn't easy." Fragmented branches, spent
petals, dried roses and the aftertaste

of broken promises. The brilliant blue
crossing the Atlantic. October's foliage

torn apart at the seams. My friends
are out west. Winds howl. I must fly home fast.

SAILING

Once a World War II naval officer,
now a Yale Law Professor dressed in old jeans,
sweat shirt, worn sneakers and crinkled hat.

He at the bow, I mid-ship, you steering
the stern, shouting-- "Lean ho." "Tack now."
and other nautical terms I've forgotten.

Our last sail out you twice lost the rudder,
sending us into a spin. Sea slapping sides.
"The damn wood's worn round the rudder."

"For God's sake, Ralph, watch what you're doing."
Fallibility and longing drew us closer.
Behind his back we winked mischievously.

Months later you drove me through the first
fierce snow. You chose a fish diner
"where the locals go." The place was packed.

Fresh scallops, beer and home-fries. "How does
it feel being. . ?" "How did you know?'
"Why it was written all over your face."

Laughing through tears we called each other
"incurable romantics." Your wit
lit up my gloom. The next day you arrived

early, though waited in your truck, wanting
to hear Beethoven's Fifth finish before driving
me to the airport. I recall your fervent

face as we kissed goodbye. You never stopped
loving music, travel, women and New York City.
Meeting him made meeting you possible.

PERSPECTIVE

A day like this one, almost balmy
after relentless storms; they say
"El Niño." At that time it was
simply "summer back east."
You grabbed a jacket. "Let's go
sailing." Geranium bowls edged
the shore of Mrs. Hall's island.
Underwater rocks and gold sluicing
sand trembling in between my toes.
Off-shore breezes. Cusps of waves
upsetting your sail-boat. Again

I'm sea-sick. Ralph is laughing
after you shout at him for dropping
the rudder and failing to tack.
Sweaty palms. A heat-wave. Thoughts
running hay-wire. A pair of swans
along the shore. Yeats believing
communion can happen even without
words as when he walked along
the cliff while Uncle George
strolled along the seashore. They
compared their intuitions at night
by the fire. Perhaps Ralph knew all
along. At the end his saying--
"Why, my dear, love was written all
over your face." That was the day
we hauled the ship ashore, tossing
a blue canvas with white ropes
over its swelling sides to keep it
safe from winter storms. And as we
tied a final knot the air smelt
faintly of lightning. Everything
went quiet. Birches, pines, birds,
hickories, aspens. Stock still
and trembling. A veil of darkness
rose past Long Island where
the Atlantic lives. Thunder roared
while we said goodbye to Ralph
by his back door. He hesitated.
His face clouding over. All this
would go unheeded. We turned away.

GERANIUMS

Red geraniums stain your porch.
I can no longer ignore
shrunken beauty, bitter regret.
Yes, sensual language can be
dangerous. You were insisting--

"Such a miracle! My finding you."
I echoing your "And I you." I thought
the forest imploded with significance--
summer's heat bursting in the maples,
paired swans circling the cove.

October flaming at its core. Quaking
aspens. Birch pods. Off-shore breezes.
The horizon went wild with clouds resembling
the day I drove you north to Bodega Bay
shrouded in thick fog while you asked me

about my affection for Balzac--
his tender understanding of women
and you insisted I ought to act with you
the way I thought he was with Eve, the woman
he loved. Your encouraging smile,

your open arms, your invitation,
yet you were the one who pivoted
at the top of the stairs
banging the storm door behind you
leaving me alone outdoors

as if on the deck of a ship that has
lost sight of the harbor or like the woman
in last night's dream retreating
through the woods, glancing back
with that look peculiar to the banished.

THE CONNECTICUT RIVER

You went on about your latest essay,
each phrase chock-full of a charm mirroring
this New England town's sense of self-

confidence as we drove through the valley
of brilliant maples towards Hartford,
past wide porched homes facing the village green.

I was mesmerized. The fog-enshrouded river
on our right reminded me of the Hudson,
the Catskills, Camp Oh-Neh-Tah set in an East

Windham valley welcoming girls from Carnarsi,
Hell's Kitchen, Redhook, Bedford-Stuyvesant,
East New York, the Bronx and Flatbush.

A region resembling Rip Van Winkle country
in my grade school reader, the Ramapos
where Richie lives, the Five Lakes region,

Lake Tiorati where Joe and I hiked after leaving
Maryknoll where my name was changed
from Carolyn to Teresita at age nineteen.

Hartford Insurance Company loomed on the left.
Mom and Dad met at Equitable Life in New York City.
They broke the company rule by dating each other.

Joe and I fell in love at Maryknoll. I miss him
more than ever. Will Stevens intercede?
Will poetry save me? Will his words

transform my distress? This State Capitol
lawn is where Stevens wrote his poems
at lunchtime. You boasted about his shyness

vanishing at the reception you hosted.
You mentioned how charming Jimmy Baldwin
was at the dinner you attended. We veered

east for your flight south. Someone was waiting.
Turning round I retraced our journey.
The Interstate fog misted my windshield.

ZURBARÁN'S NEW YORK VISIT

Quite accidentally I found Zurbarán's name
lettered in white on a maroon banner.
"You're my lucky charm,
always finding the things I love."

Inside you pointed to Francis of Assisi
whose dusty cowl almost hid his face and hands.
I thought him strangely sensual.
We paused at Saint Cecilia costumed

in a blue peasant blouse and red skirt,
as she offered her eyes on a tray for God.
Your penetrating blue gaze went over
her figure. You flicked your wrist

before a Madonna and child, knowing
this sort of gesture "turned me on."
"See how the child mirrors the mother's
full lips and dark wide-apart eyes."

(Did I, did you, did we ever think of
being parents together?) Your growing
flamboyance, my increasing inhibition.
You called John the Baptist "precious"

as he reached for Christ's foot.
You drew me near Anne who embraced
her daughter and grandson in an arc
of protective understanding. (You've

yet to meet my mother.) You set each
painting in its proper historical epoch.
You enjoyed talking about the details
of your story, listened less and less

to mine. Were your complaints about ageing
a smokescreen. Now and again your words
about the woman who wanted a family.
She also loved you. What was I

to do? Was I guilty of mixing Eros's
arrows with Sebastian's? You praised
"Saint Peter's restraint." This sounded
like preaching. When frightened

I worried. "Zurbarán's subjects are natural,
subtle, unforced." How stay calm in
the face of your insistence on style,
form, discretion. She was free of

family ties. "Don't ask questions!"
My Flatbush forwardness strictly
forbidden. Only "yes," "wow," "of course,"
permitted. You stared past my awkward

need for reassurance. Each martyr
survived defeat, thanks to sainthood.
Is there one who will advise me wisely?
"Give up, go home. Don't be afraid."

Your "ah, ah" at the monk's inner flame
concealed by cloak and cowl. I feared
losing your friendship altogether.
We sizzled, flared, smoldered,

drawn to and shocked by Saint
Lawrence grilled on both sides.
We found Agatha's breasts on a platter,
not a drop of blood in sight.

Where is her agony, where her oppressor?
Was my psyche scattered over this
gallery floor? Someone somewhere else
orchestrates my departure. You say

"I can't stand blood or gore in art."
Is the soul bloodied when wounded?
Can betrayal alter love's language?
My mistake began at the entrance--

believing Gabriel's open arms signified
"good news," so I ignored the angel
at the exit warning of "downfall"
where two guards forbid re-entry.

BRÜNNHILDE AT THE FRICK

Cabs, cars, trucks on Madison Avenue.
Sweltering heat subsides
following thunder and lightning.

"Water Music" fills the courtyard.
A bronze angel touches his lips.
Palm plants and air conditioning.

Silence broken by a woman in a pink
jogging suit and pink sneakers.
She dangles a gold necklace

as she dramatizes Brünnhilde's
dilemma. The man beside her nods.
She ignores Wotan's warning--

"Don't disobey. Don't save the lovers."
A father's rage, a daughter's courage.
Passion. Disobedience. Daring.

Love. Loyalty. Opposition.
Am I beyond help? Have I wandered
too far? How save myself?

Three times I stood for San Francisco
Opera's "Ring," soon falling for
a similar Siegfried's irresistible charm.

Now we're to meet at the Plaza bar.
Torn by duty. Tormented by desire.
Outcome cloudy. Brünnhilde risks

her life for Sieglinde, so suffers
Wotan's scorn. Such a fierce
father figure. If Siegfried lies

she'll seek revenge. The leitmotif
is churning-- love's dangerous
potion drawn. Wotan's fiery circle

protects his daughter-- only a hero
shall wake her, even if Valhalla
falls. The stakes are high. My future

sails on stormy seas. A boom-box
blares for rappers across the street
by Central Park. Will I face the music

and slay the dragon my anima
adores. Should I burn all
our letters all at once? He suggests

champagne and pretzels, waving
his handkerchief at the finale.
Brünnhilde's braver by far--

turning all she lost into the ring
she set on fire. Our final walk
round the flaming tulips

in the cloister garden peering into
their dark smoldering cores.
I'll fly west. Jet propulsion.

ACROSS FROM CENTRAL PARK

The Magdalene sits in a darkened room
pondering her fate not far from

the golden Virgin who ascends
bodily to heaven opposite Central Park.

"Her kind will not be seen again." says
one woman to another as they stand

watching Vermeer's yellow robed woman
who turns towards someone who

offers her a letter she's afraid to open.
Perhaps at lunch these women will

discuss what they know and don't know
about love. Knowing loss in advance

doesn't ease its ache, or alter the outcome.
Diana pivots at the middle of an adjoining room.

Her Achilles' heel exposed. She is aiming
her arrow at an unseen adversary

or hidden lover. Have I sent myself
conflicting messages-- stay, leave,

hold on, let go. Bob's kindness in playing
"Dutch Uncle" back in California--

"Take this in by way of information."
Magdalene holds the mirror sideways

as she gazes into the dark. Some say
she spent her last years in a cave overlooking

southern France. Maybe Verdi used Magdalene
for "Leonora" in "La Forza del Destino."

My faith falters. I've never accepted the fact
of my father dying young. This was his

favorite museum-- Bellini's Francis
of Assisi, Holbein's Thomas More,

El Greco's Jerome. I use this courtyard
as a church, trying to gather my courage.

A medieval angel points in a direction
I can't decipher. An Ingres woman

in a gray taffeta dress and red bow
smiles confidently above the ferns.

I'm far from possessing her composure.
Neither do I know Diana's daring

independence. I've returned to the city
of my birth, as after leaving the cloister,

this time to salvage a friendship
that's proven disastrous. What can I

say to my son whose majoring in Theater
Arts at Fordham's Lincoln Center.

He insists-- "You don't need this guy."
I try telling him I never stopped loving

his father. My words sound hollow.
He doesn't know I've promised

his brother "I'll be back in California
by January." I need closure

on my own, not by phone. Both sons
frame my dilemma, the word I need

is "No" after "Yes" has happened.
Hasn't Hegel helped me before--

his drawing opposites together,
his *go with the flow* into unforseen

places. How Magdalene faced
Jesus in the garden, wanting to

touch him but being told "No."
"I must go." "Come again. Come

again. You will, won't you?"
"Yes." "No." "Maybe." "Who can

say?" All this uncertainty swirls
in my heart. The woman in yellow

is about to open the letter. Magdalen
sees past the painter. Diana runs

for fun. The woman in gray taffeta
keeps her secret. My sons are back

in the Bay Area. I live with their father
not far from them. The past is scattered

over the city where both my parents
were born-- Brooklyn, New York.

THE STATE CAPITAL

Clear, brisk maple leaves applaud
that October afternoon,
as if they knew your 737 would soon

touch down from Milwaukee, Wisconsin
to Hartford, Connecticut. Our phone
lines had crinkled for weeks.

You being an H.D. scholar,
both of us romantics, we evoked
Eros and Mercury his messenger.

I waited at Gate 77, pressed
against the grey terminal wall,
watching you enter the lobby.

My nervous, anxious, hopeful "Hi."
Driving back to my rented cottage
we conjured Lawrence's ghost,

hoping he'd influence favorable
odds this one weekend that we
promised an undying friendship.

After you flew home I scanned
the pier we walked in driving rain,
your words tossed about

by the tail-end of a storm,
crossing my mind's memory,
ears ringing with loss.

THE GREEN

She sent her Dorsoduro address too late,
the letter arriving after we left. Yet,
her accompanying presence in Venice,
where her mother played the violin

by an open window. We met accidentally
at the Pound conference. I noticed her
in the crowd, not knowing who she was,
yet struck by her strong, intelligent face.

(Later reading *Discretions* I learned
she knew four languages since childhood).
Quite by accident, we crossed High Street
together. She invited me to breakfast

overlooking "the green." We spoke of love's
disappointments, its loss and the endless
work of being a mother, daughter, a poet.
On the third day we hugged by the library,

breaths visible in an early October frost.
She smiled at my seeking her face for a sign.
"Now don't idolize me, I'm only human.
In the end you'll see, it's worthwhile."

Her poem arrived about "the green"
signifying a hidden loss. She ended
by saying-- "Take heart, your poems love you.
They'll companion you throughout life."

THE OWL OF MINERVA

The owl of Minerva gathers her wings
at the closing of dusk.

          - Hegel

"What happened? An infatuation?"
"I suppose so." Having dressed carefully
for lunch the day he introduced
you who saved my life.

October's stars sprinkled hope
after such an early snow. "If only
once more . . . " I pleaded

in Milwaukee on my way home west.
"Will we meet again?" "No, never.
Remember, I'm only your doorway."
"Please. Just one more weekend."

A year later you met someone
at your college. "Congratulations."
"Yes, she's quite wonderful.

We're very happy." "You know I want
your happiness. The shore we walked
towards the sea. Did you notice?"
"Notice what?" "How much you mattered?"

"Yes, of course. But you must
go on, find your own happiness.
Go forward. Have confidence."

Corresponding across a continent.
"I believe in you." "And I in you."
Such a healing tonic, your "ah ,
ah," worked wonders. I miss

your owl-like wings gliding,
your encouraging cadences,
your "Bless you." My "You too."

H.D.

> *No traveler is free from seaweed. Myrtle*
> *Grows near, dense with bi-colored fruit; a cavern*
> *Lies in the grove, made, possibly by nature,*
> *By art, more likely.*
> - Ovid, *Metamorphoses*, "The Story of Thetis"

Oh, H.D., my sister in those days
when the myrtle thickened the cliffs
and you ran on ahead of Richard,
your sandal slipping, so you cut your foot
and he handed you violets placed on the pillow,
the same day you felt the sea-breeze in your hair.
It was summer in Greece, England, Connecticut.
Sail-boats dotted the cove. You caught sight
of his sea-blue eyes and she of all your friends
had the courage to warn you. Wasn't she called
Bryher? Already it was too late to recover
July's intensity. The screen doors were removed,
the potted plants taken indoors and you thought
yourself foolish to go on loving him
in the same room he made love to someone else,
though just in time your life was saved as you
learned to let go of what was intimately
savored. Still you cannot forget the green slopes
leading to the sea, nymphs playing in the surf,
reeds thick with shore-birds, paired swans landing
inside the ring made salty by the Sound. Don't
say it wasn't worth your all. Threads woven
into the text may be deciphered years later.
You sip tea in the Swiss garden, hear a voice
echoing down the corridor whose cadence is
familiarly encoded in the sparks your body
knows by heart, deeper than consciousness

not hope, since you shall never meet him again,
yet sight, sound and touch alive and entering,
the way hands, lips, eyes and skin remember . . .

THE CLOISTERS, HENRY HUDSON DRIVE

for my father, Edwin A. Cook 1915-1966

Basil, lavender, rosemary, marjoram, thyme.
Monks are singing the Hour of Terce.

Torches of sunlight flare in the corners.
Dad calls us-- "Richie, Carolyn, John!"

We're running through the Cloister halls,
hiding behind pillars. Years later a phone-call

out west will bring me back east to comfort
a widower. I'll arrange candles and violets

for his table and visit The Cloisters
where a medieval angel on the left

raises his arm with a warning-- "Avoid fear.
Avoid attachment. Find the middle."

Joseph Campbell's words on the Bill Moyers'
video I carried with me to Connecticut.

Where is "the middle?" The rotunda with William
Carlos Williams contemplating the unicorn

lady as a centerpiece to his *Patterson* poem,
so weaving his affection for New Jersey

women into his work. Is she afraid
an unseen archer will slay her beloved

animal? In San Francisco my friend Neil
counsels his patients to recover their animal

nature. A Jungian, he apparently
believes, as Thomists and Buddhists do,

in a middle way, modulating extreme
differences. Love can play havoc

or lead to healing. My memory's brushed
with falling flakes of melting snow

under the lamppost outside our Brooklyn
rented rooms. Dad pulls the sleigh

to the hill near the boathouse overlooking
Prospect Park Lake-- "Go Carolyn go!

Steer down the middle." I hesitated.
"Be brave. You can do it!"

Quick as a flash, I flew from his side
into the cold night air, bumping on rocks

all the way down to the lake's icy edge
where my brothers were waiting.

After Dad died I've avoided Brooklyn.
Do the places loved by those we've

loved still carry their presence?
Does the past seep into the present?

Leaning on the ledge facing the Palisades
I watch the maples dripping rain

on to the handkerchief of the Hudson
River as it flows below Maryknoll's

Sunset Hill, where I spent my early
twenties as a novice and later met Joe

above Manhattan and the borough
of Brooklyn, where I was born.

IV

Here the past and the present
fused, and her own life, with its
trivial devices and desires, seemed
only an insignificant moment in
the long history of the headland.

-P. D. James

EMILE NOLDE (1867-1956)

(i) "TWO WOMEN"

Two women stand in for
my past and present, having again
    returned to this shore.

A green peninsular stretches
past the waves and boarded-up homes
    towards a dark blue horizon.

One woman says she understands;
the other stays quiet.
    More experienced, she knows better

than her naive sister.
Belief and loss brought them back
    after an abrupt departure.

Would the man's presence balance things?
Actually he created this rift
    to begin with, better off without him.

Have they found understanding?
Their postures suggest puzzlement,
    even shock. Perhaps resignation.

A deserted green plain
holding sea, shore, sky
    and two women leaning on each other.

(ii) "ROUGH SEAS"

This yellow horizon inhales thunderous
lightning. Two ships are drawing close.
One slows. The other surges. Silence
looms. No message. Not even "goodbye."

Was someone trying to say-- "Don't leave."
Tidal interlacings. Competitive currents.
Merciful retreating tides. High rising
crests. Storms eroding the shore-line.

One vessel veers sideways avoiding contact.
The other stays still, then recedes.
Radar cannot detect what is being
written under the surface, below deck.

(iii) "SUNFLOWERS AND ZINNIAS"

A blue core emitting black sparks,
since he has gone.   A yellow fan
fails calm the bursting petal's
confusion. Tears burrow. Brown fur
hides in clusters. Red contractions.
Tossed aside, she tried to please.
Open faced, the single zinnia falls
sideways in the storm. Such dismissal
stings. Flattery shines round those
prized specimens admired indoors.
Yesterday's glory split at the seams.
Will hope survive the winter? Seeds,
if dried, may scatter summer's orange
red and yellow stained memory.

(iv) "POPPIES"

1.

Flamed petals gloss over their secrets.
Dark filaments weep. Rain streaks across
the turbulent sea. Violet shadows gather.

Pink clouds rush away. Each bloom has
finished. All that's left is to forget
what a summer it was. Fiery smoke
screens the night's delirious charm
when love thrived on figments of
imagination, till the dust settled
along an unpredictably dark horizon.
Rusty fog, ghostly recriminations.
A black cored poppy rustles in moonlight.

2.

Dark filaments whisked by air.
Teasing purple undersides fail
to revive. Residues of pollen
in your blood-stream. Memory's
smoke-screen. Trying to undo
the harm that's done. Layer on
layer of "yes" tossed aside.
Certain syllables never spoken.
"Sorry" is a word you must say to
those who wait. Dawn can't erase
a night's delirious charm or how
a pink crescent moon trembles
on each scarlet leaf. He carved
initials on the hickory by his door.
You'll never know if he remembers.

(v) "SEEBULL"

A yellow sky seeps past
this northern farmhouse. Left behind
you travel back, believing your steps
matter, that his hands might shape
an oval opening again. Promontory
where sea, sky, and shore originate.
A bluish road facing a secret, dark door.

Twilight, violet birds
circling rain-clouds. Yellow gray
lines. Never again near enough to hear
your breath. Never again your hands
opening and closing. What might have been
may haunt us yet at the sky and sea's
nearby ledge. A blue vault left over . . .

VITA, VIRGINIA

Vital words. Exotic food. A Persian moon
caressing Gordon Square. Midnight hesitations.
Howling wind. Why is she now so far from me?
Golden October's magenta blanket. Dogs,
horses, her country house, the morning fog,
rose garden and rolling moors. Barn swallows,
a shadowy attic, dusty roses. Summer sweat
with Vita by my side. The stream going on
and on after she's gone. Pages. Voices. Disguises.
Another regretful telegram. Husbands, children.
Who is laughing with her the way she did with me?
Doubt. Fear. Who is this Violet? Will it ever end?
Alone in my study remembering our *Orlando*.

RENOIR'S OBSESSION

Near the end Renoir confided to his grandson--
"I have painted the same three or four pictures all my life.
If breasts hadn't existed, I'd never have painted figures.
They're enough to make you fall on your knees before their beauty."
I'm not surprised, having guessed his obsession half-way
through the exhibition, repeatedly drawn to these figures
as his painting this woman at the opera, a startling
intimacy expressed in the purpose her blue dress sheathes,

setting off such fine shoulders, brownish-red hair
tied in a knot, eyes half closed. She teases, withdraws,
pretends, hiding the pleasure she possesses as she
observes being observed, making it impossible for us
not to stop, stare and enjoy how strands of pearls glimmer
over her breasts, how silk sounds rise round her figure,
how beads of sweat gather on her forehead. Seemingly
embarrassed she fans her throat, withdrawing her gaze
as if we intrude on a private moment hanging in the balance
between our attentions and Renoir's intentions convincing me
she is flattered by this sitting for his sake, her sake,
our sake, how he brings bright color to her cheeks.

YES, MARK ROTHKO

one Thursday evening
I found Mark Rothko's
paintings in SF-MOMA

having climbed the granite stairs
leading into the space
filling the silence of his soul

and now the morning after
with my eyes closed
black wash is speaking

beside violet blue
hum   hum   hum
a layered humming

color articulating form
moving toward consent
a surprising twist

of yellow red bands
I've bedded down with
orange penetrating blue

giving rise to an unquenchable
thirst for more sun kissed
eyelids veiling songs

of yes to your vision
you and more than you
a canvas   a world

a fragrant virile
forest blue deepening
the substance of black

without blindness
this blessing of violet
covenanting yellow

green crossing a white sheet
hidden in plum lips
forgiving everything

needy as natural
aged by mid-night splashes
praying on the borders

of barely visible pink
longing   such surprising
cobalt blue darkening bliss

FINDING YOU IN SAN FRANCISCO, MARK ROTHKO

behind the large orange space
a faint rectangular undertow
consciously pulsing with
body and soul clothed
by oil pigments that sing
infinitely towards
a horizontal blue expanding
up down and sideways

so the ladder keeps climbing
with what he has become
in his creation having
created him   he looks
through the frame saying
"such a high in California
. . . light bouncing back
saturated by sea and sky."

rain soaked green parallel
to the chartreuse wonder
of childhood shoe laces
and July bleaching the hair
on bare arms plus this fuzzy
underside of longing
suggested by stretching
yellow horizontally

or flattening haystacks
in a field going off into
final white while the paint
hums and humming comes
alive within black's
smaller vertical notes
hiding half-way inside
the valley of delight

provoking his presence
inside this medium he has
invented to express him-
self as you me we us
when the sun's lemony sweet
when roses spill wide pink sleeves
when blue's used only on special occasions
when violet's velvet and rough on skin

each stroke made actual
self-contained and combining

such discreet flickering shadows
throughout these rooms intensifying
the exhibition's mood as the museum
guard guesses my wish to take
this painting home since soon
someone will take it away

PAULA MODERSOHN-BECKER (1876-1907)

(i) PAULA AND RILKE

Your colors meld, then separate out
into dreams, dances, sleep, love-making,
cornflowers in a girl's brown hair.
I whisper-- "sister, sister, sister."

You respond-- "It's not the struggle,
but isolation in the provinces.
Urgency forms my body's work--
fruit, flower, tree, child, lover,

these things I can't relinquish."
How near he was when you left
your self-portrait-- nude to the waist,
a camellia over your heart,

your belly swollen with child.
Your soul visible on the canvas.
He came close to tasting.
You made his work possible,

calming his fear of death,
whenever he called--
"woman, woman, woman."
He sought your source.

Unweaned, he drank from
your presence, so that in dying
you became his confidante
making the nights

less lonely. He conjured
your laughter under the oak trees,
your stirring soup in the kitchen,
your playing with boys by the river.

He evoked your shade
for as long as necessary,
placing your intensity carefully
inside his lines and stanzas.

(ii) PATRONAGE

Often wearing chic dresses and gold wrist bands
these women write letters, send stipends, invitations.
Princess Maria insists-- "Stay at my Duino castle."
In August, Frau Hertha's-- "Come to my Munich home,

compose under Picasso's *La Famille des Saltimbanques*."
Roses, an oak desk, a comfortable chair. You face
Orpheus in the garden among willows. Breakfast on a tray.
Pick up your pen. Forget your friend. Leave her alone.

Such fine food, interesting music, all expenses paid
including a travel allowance and your work sustained
by admiring women, who tip-toe outside your study.
A ready audience-- who could ask for anything more.

Vintage wine poured. Violin serenades on the terrace.
Paula ought to understand, after all, time is precious,
your work is absorbing, no hours left over.
If her confidence should weaken, that's unfortunate.

Sharing your friends is another matter. Besides
she has never asked directly. Suggest she leave Paris,
return to her family in the country, paint when possible.
Avoiding wife and daughter, you pursue art relentlessly.

(iii) YOUR LETTER

Your handwriting on the envelope made
my heart race. I read the letter
under the almond branches,
slowly resaying each syllable
as you came alive in the contours
my lips gave your cadences.

We wondered if our nearness was born
in a refusal to name God in the old ways--
a white bearded man hidden in heaven.
We preferred an attendant silence
on the edge of an apple orchard.

You gave up wife and child for poetry.
I was pulled back by others,
expected to forget myself for them.
Ignoring convention, you gave yourself to art.
Do you remember our last day in Paris,
side by side, not far from the river

your being absorbed in the statue
of Apollo, while I believed
his magnificent form resembled yours.
Then you waved goodbye at the train station.
I headed north, back to Otto in Germany.

(iv) MIDNIGHT

She fell back stunned at his change
since having opened herself to
his advancing strength,
not fearing the diminishment

he dreaded, nor his worry
about being lost in love,
though his hesitations hurt
her spontaneity and courage,

so he tore the veils off her his anima
by refusing to brave their differences,
ridiculing her trying so hard.
He fled her silvery shadows,

the darkened pools that both
attracted and unnerved him.
Such way-stations must be avoided.
Free, above all else,

he must be free to strike out
on his own, while she felt
sacrifice need not decrease the self.
Quick-silver he came, so shall go.

THE WHITENESS OF FRANZ MARC

what whiteness will you add to this whiteness, what candor?
. . . . . .and a white ox on the road toward Pisa
-Ezra Pound, *Canto LXXIV*

I will add the lovely hands of Franz Marc
at a cafe table in Vienna as he picks up
the blue and white porcelain coffee cup
slowly bringing it to his lips.

Is he the continent's counterpart to Rupert Brooke--
free, urbane, charming, "a back-to-nature man"
whose broad forehead shelters sensitive dark eyes.
"Do not leave, do not leave."

Mounting his white horse he believes this
changes the future. On entering the green forest
a doe eagerly awaits his touch,
two blond sun-shafts warm his flesh.

Now in August I need him intensely.
A cafe table draped with a white and blue cloth
along a city street where he was photographed.
Why his early exit, why that wasteful war?

Plane trees in heavy disbelieving foliage . . .
Will I see him lift the white cup to his lips,
touch his long beautiful fingers,
feel the fiery glance of his contemplative eyes.

I pretend his paintings insist he is not lost
to us forever. I caress the brown doe,
reddish fox, blue horse, the dark green shadows
and orange spotted white ox.

This exercise on a white page, setting the table
with white cloth and blue cup anticipates his return,
seeing his black hair, dark eyes, sensual mouth,
and the fragile whiteness of his naivete.

MY ANIMUS FOX, FRANZ MARC

You guessed her love for blue
surrounded by green and yellow.
You understood the tan doe's
curved neck signifying privacy.

Again you created a potent space
for shy desires-- what was lost
repeatedly sought salvation.
You deepened shadows, parting

light-shafts that pierced a pine grove.
You held her closely in view,
brush ready for bleached muslin.
You knew her situation,

having been there before;
perhaps you never left,
so you made the soul a small,
tender, brilliant fox,

naming him her "animus,"
laughing as you highlighted
his reddish fur with a white tail.
"Ah," you said, "here is my gift

skirting about a loam green bed.
Make yourself at home where I
play with the purple tints
of your dark hair leaning over me."

V

The manuscript which reposed
above her heart began shuffling
and beating, as if it were a living thing . . .

- Virginia Woolf

Not to destroy,
nay but to sanctify
each flame
that springs
upon the brow of Love

- H. D.

APOLLO

You've returned, winged spirit,
having partnered my hopes and losses,
not forgetting that summer of your sudden

appearance after the storm. I reached
for your hand. Poplars were swaying
on the horizon. Water was pulsing

by our feet. We found the hawthorne
hedges alive with pink and white buds.
Wasn't it you who tried to warn me?

Everything in the forest felt charged
with meaning. Who was the messenger?
Who possessed the words to charm?

Who stood silently where the road divided?
Was Dante alone when he entered
the dark woods? Was Beatrice always

waiting? My hands try reshaping each
significance-- were my caresses ablutions
or anointments? If so, for what purpose?

Would my voice fail, if I lost self-
confidence? Will my ego stand
again after it falls? Stunned by lightning

I sought your burning figure under
the waterfall where nymphs were
playing hide-and-go-seek the day

I discovered lilies of the valley alongside
his driveway and red berries shining
with sweetness that last morning.

The swans disappeared at twilight.
Maple trees were shedding their golden
leaves on the lawn as I tried to focus

beyond the present into a past hiding
my future. Then you lent me
the vision of poplars lining the horizon

at sunset, hoping the threads of my psyche
would knit together as I traced
the coppery lines filming your body,

while you smiled at my impulsive nature.
Blue-green guppies tickled our legs.
Humidity on your lips and forehead.

Your sun warmed head, shoulders, arms,
chest, hips, legs, ankles, toes. Porpoises
round your chariot. Light became a torch

heating the canal all the way west. Lavender
edged the forest. The boy Pan was playing
his flute. Your kindly gaze, your healing hands.

ACTUAL GRACE (Della Robbia's "Prudence")
for James Merrill

she held the mirror
in her right hand partially hiding the shade who stood behind
ardently breathing
a warning for Eurydice not to believe her climb out of Hades
signified an actual ascent
rather a pretense staged by a shadowy figure who cleverly
toured in disguises
misconstruing Orpheus's call not leading towards salvation
so back she'll fall

losing the sheen gold gives when dissolved in the bloodstream
                         for healing
since she offered more than sympathy and he promised friendship
                         only to drop her
the month he refused to attend her New York City reading
                         thus fear rose
in her voice having just heard "I can't come" her friends never
                         knew the challenge
arriving by phone tearing love's last threaded spell woven
                         round her psyche
as a protective cloak so this struggle not to sink into self-
                         pity saved by a gallant
man who offered tea roasted almonds erudite language toasting
                         life's ups and downs
celebrating love being comparable to religion in its devotion
                         to another believing
things may turn around after all such resurrections do happen
                         why not surrender to
the green serpent who weaves Plato's golden mean through
                         the woman's fingers
over her middle defeating death with sky blue white waves
                         curving round her waist
bordered by grapes pears lemons apples vines and avocadoes
                         sun-trumpets announcing
the one served by songs who came rather close is succeeded
                         by another more
gracious and kind in a Manhattan home when through tears
                         she spilled her story
beginning in Brooklyn about an artistic father dying young
                         as he listened
mirroring back her loss this gentleman whose hospitality
                         banished regret
setting free the Spirit through casual pleasantries
                         tongued fire
and unassuming what Aquinas long ago named *actual grace*

ANNUNCIATION

He wears sandals similarly worn by Mercury.
Golden feathers slowly stir. She is studying
the Scriptures. Suddenly the sound of his beating
wings makes her jump. Supplicant, proud, unsure.
A single lily held in his hand. Fire flickers
under his heavy lids. Strong reserved shoulders
and bold glances. Is he playing the fool?
What to say? What to do? Violets tremble
in the hem of their clothes. Breathing close,
his fingers glaze her forehead. Planets moving
round the sun. Tides of the moon overtaking
the shore. Reaching for the lily she smiles
not knowing her "yes" will make him vanish.

VISITATION (ATGET, Versailles)

I found him in the old San Francisco
Museum of Modern Art. An exhibition
devoted to Atget. He was struggling
in the shade as he set his tripod in place.
A breeze ruffled the edges of his coat.
He pulled his scarf closer around his neck.
The garden was damp and musty. Dawn had just
begun to move across the tips of wet plane leaves.
His eye was drawn to the shutter, a magnet going for
iron, his hands, soul, mind and heart pleading
for minute substances to adhere inside the shadows
and light composing the scene. He drew Pan
into focus as he lifted his flute, close
to his lips. He noticed the beads of moisture
flowing down the god's slender shoulder.
He was fond of the half-smile where shade
gave way to brilliant light. Several tries
were made at capturing his beauty.
He returned home with the plates warm

in his jacket. This says nothing
about the labor later with chemicals
in the darkness, the fumes, sweat,
dizziness each time he clipped the damp
substance and hung it to dry, waiting
anxiously, then opening the door slowly.
The shock, disbelief, wonder as he
carefully cut each piece away from
the other in this subterranean chamber--
his isolated endeavor, his secret
alchemic feat and, if lucky, such
pleasure exploding in his hands
as he held the frame up to the light--
the young god-child Pan as he was
when he found him that August morning
in the pre-dawn shadows as the first
rays of the sun touched his shoulders.

ORPHEUS AND EURYDICE

Seven streams rippling through the forest
that summer my life emerged alongside yours,
a single spring, hidden by pines and plane trees,
sending itself into underground channels, bubbling
into a basin of silvery fish circling a green wall, a triple-
tiered fountain lifting the darkness into light as Orpheus
calls Eurydice again and again as she swims through the canal
past the rose garden then disappears suddenly as a cloud releases
rain, an arrow tears across the sky falling to earth and you say
this is a sign Iris gives those who play in regions bordering
heaven and earth, night and day, loving and letting-go,
caressing and waving goodbye, your words drawing
close and receding, conjuring love's magic potion
the way our parents did, reinventing hope,
making us happen as Eurydice sings by
Orpheus' ear, their emerging in light.

ANCESTORS

. . . I answer for my ancestors the questions
that their lives once left behind. - Carl G. Jung

Behind the house, a garden's damp
liquidy light inside each chestnut's core.

A rusty gate swings open. Shadows pass through.
Fish are rubbing the basin's silvery gods.

Heat, clustering roses, silky
flamed cores. Evaporation happens.

Gray weather-beaten vases accompanying
nymphs and dryads. I ran across the lawn

to meet you. Blackened birches were
warning. I ignored their presence.

Church bells rang across the river.
I touched your future head-stone.

My past tore away without consent.
The life I knew began breaking in two.

Who could revive my weakened will?
Minerva, Diana or the wise virgin?

July's photo shows us side by side,
my hand naively pressing yours.

We walked arm-in-arm by stunning dahlias.
Our intimacy would haunt me later.

Were kisses worth such anguish?
A water lily's supplicating call.

Wine sipped outdoors. Ancestral spirits
stir, the seal of silence broken.

HERMES

> *"Hermes," the divine messenger, brings the message*
> *of destiny . . .*   - Martin Heidegger

A large basin, plane trees, elms,
maples and orange trees deifying

February's monarch butterflies. Rough
stones house green guppies circling

the edge. Certain things are asked.
I can't deceive myself anymore;

he is gone. The underground fountain is
silent. Cascading roses are spent.

The heart-shaped violets have vanished.
"Come home. Come home." We never

said goodbye. What happened
happened whether I liked it or not,

the way drought followed
last winter's relentless storms,

leaving the summer a tinder-box,
so fires ravaged California's wilderness,

though the redwoods survived,
native plants reseeded and Julia Butterfly

saved a tree called *Luna* from the loggers,
and a friend offered his cabin on the Point Reyes

peninsula, so comforted by pines
and manzanitas, I happened on a pamphlet

telling the story of *Women's Initiation
Rites at Pompeii* where a mural shows

a woman hesitating in the middle
of a room as a winged figure of Hermes

waves a staff towards her while
three women bring bowls of water

and a man is about to open a basket
awakening my dream of a golden child

the night before an abandoned animal
appeared in my garden and the words

of Marion Woodman came to mind--
how such things portent shifts

in the psyche; this golden furred creature
who purrs, *Hermes, messenger of change.*

ANIMUS

i.

Wondering if the one I used to love
was an Orphean figure? Or am I confusing

Mary with Eurydice (to say nothing of Psyche).
She waits by the window overlooking

the green. He is rushing towards me,
up close and flattering. I'm flabbergasted.

Such a dashing figure, the same age
as my deceased father. Why now? What's

next on the horizon? I'm not free.
He insists he is inexperienced and lonely.

ii.

Pauline reads aloud her recurrent dream.
This time on her eighty-sixth birthday

she lies on the sea-bed watching a man sail
nearby. She wants him to reach down

and carry her. He veers away. She sees
her mother atop a familiar Washington peak.

"You must climb. Come Pauline. I'm waiting."
She tells us women how at age forty-two

she met her father for the first time
since he left the family when she was twelve.

They sat on a park bench facing the sea.
That was the last time she saw him alive.

As a Wac during WW II she nursed
the wounded, then taught poor kids

in Brooklyn's Bedford Stuyvesant
and in San Francisco's Richmond

near the ocean. She adores Jung's work,
insisting he saved her life. Pauline's

dream proved not to be a premonition
about dying, since at ninety-four she's still

writing about how happy she was as a child in Washington before the age of twelve.

Penni thinks Pauline's dream is "archetypal, each woman's search for her animus."

VI

One must do something about the past.
It doesn't just cease to be. It goes on
existing and affecting the present, and in
new and different ways, as if in some other
dimension it too were growing.

- Iris Murdoch

CHRIST AT HAND

(Tintoretto, Scuola San Rocco, Venice)

A small mirror, rented at the entrance,
draws Christ from the ceiling into my hands.

Prisms turn him every which way,
a muscular figure leaving the mountain top.

Transfiguration or Ascension?
We slowly make our way down this huge hall,

rounding a corner where we find him
completely alone, except for the brooding

judge seated in the shadows who
seems unable to turn away from this bereft

figure awaiting his sentence.
A tattered robe hangs off his bare shoulders.

His large constricted chest evokes desire
and grief at such vitality soon seen

crucified in the next alcove.
All church furnishings are absent.

I cannot light a candle or bring roses.
No kneelers, no vases, no mourners,

no friends in sight and yet we know
there were a few who stayed faithful

to the end. What a shock finding him
in the next room at a glorious homecoming,

this magnificent man swimming among angels
and while gazing at him I'm thinking of

your agonies and glory and this need
we have to be held, healed and resurrected.

CHAGALL'S WINDOW, STRASBOURG

The war blew out your stained glass windows
and tore the infant from your arms. Now the dove's

wide wings beat again above your heart. Reds
brighten the background of your dark blue dress.

Yellow and green trees dance. Palm leaves
breathe by your side. Chagall has given you

an ordinary chair to be your throne. On this,
the eve of the Assumption, the last rays of sunlight

flood the vestibule as Peruvian flute music
mixes with bells echoing across the city.

A blind woman in a simple flowered dress grips
the pew. "Yahweh," she sings, "You know me

when I lie down, and when I stand." She whispers
the words that will change bread and wine

into Christ's body and blood. With eyes closed
she slowly makes her way toward the sanctuary

touching the raised edge of each pew. Her face
appears radiant as she turns to leave, singing

the final hymn, reminding me of the way
I used to be for the God who would be mine.

CHARTRES

In returning to this beloved place
I'm reminded of how Marguerite Yourcenar's
love for Hadrian opened the past as a healing
balm the way it may happen at Chartres
where the Virgin, hidden in the shadows,
is a blazing presence when the morning sun
changes granite to ruby, topaz and violet
as the side door opens and the zephyr flies in
saying "I know, I know. Long ago women
sought shelter in this sanctuary, hearing
the bell echo in the lower chamber three times,
while the terra cotta wall traces the figure
of Mary and her Child during the consecration
as the red wine melts on the white cloth
brought to their lips and the scent of incense,
fennel, wheat fields and roses mix by the back door,
chestnut trees fanning themselves in the shadows
below the jewel of seven Spirits darting in
and out the heart's circumference since kneeling
is not a shameful thing. "Yes" is a sound
the candles make as the match strikes
their core. Nothing is lost. No. Never.
She will not turn away, neither will the divine
child in her arms, their dual throne is among
the oldest in this world, their red, black
and burnt-sienna figures gazing at you
across the shoulder of Judas, who will betray
her son, but here, they are protected from harm."

MONT SAINT MICHEL

Last summer's blue-grey roof and tower
in the afternoon August sun. What will I
say when you are gone. Again I'll seek
your voice in a crowd. Sweet inflections
and silence turning over in my heart later on,

knowing you also love these galloping tides,
gull cries, the Vesper bell, street lamps, cafes,
winding stairs, damp cobblestones. Your hands
pressed the shutters. They opened and closed.
At Mass we tasted the same bread and wine
of Christ's transubstantiated body and blood.
Transfixed, oh Love, Love's tongued fire.

PROVENCE, LES SAINTES MARIES

for Joseph

Traveling round the Bay the train hugs
the curved shore and the sky appears to have
stepped into the tree-tops. All sense of loss
subsides since sunlight is up-close and flooding
these olive orchards and your words are watching
over my writing, the good and the bad alike,
as you always will and I bask in your warmth
the way I have for years on other shores,
though first I enter the town's white-washed
chapel whose crypt houses Saint Sarah's shrine,
patroness of gypsies in whose company countless
candles are ignited, so many the entire chamber hums
and the humming is a prayer as my heart hums too
for you, saying your name over and over
though no one hears except yourself
and I think the kind spirits are caressing
my face as I cry since you have gone and I go
afterwards across the crowded noisy plaza
through a thicket of tourists, past the food
stalls to the warm bright sand and strip
to the waist as most women do on this beach
and standing somewhat self-conscious
yet determined I swim nude in the Mediterranean
pretending I'm Aphrodite's sister, born to love
and looking back to the shore I see you waving.

PARIS, JOURNEY HOME

Along the boulevard in August humidity
rises from the pavement. You decided to come
before I asked you. We were sipping café au lait.
The heat of the day inside your hands. I wanted
to kiss you. All around us glasses were clinking.
Cars were humming. Lovers were whispering.
Side by side the plane trees of the St-Germaine
de-Près garden deep in sleep. Love became
a friend of the saint for whom you lit a candle
at lunchtime. All was not lost, even after
we left. Not far away the Arc de Triomphe was
suffused by the setting sun. We held our breath
after dark where the Place de la Concorde's
liquid pulse was arching over Neptune's
nymphs at the stroke of midnight. Inflections
of Latin, French and English at the Mass
offered for a safe journey home. I found
the dark red roses outside the church door,
their tissued bodies covered in glory.

BENEDICTION, AVEBURY

Maple trees in their golden foliage along
the border circling Brooklyn's Grand Plaza
on the edge of Park Slope where grandma
prepared for the sun every season and strolled
Prospect Park till she waved to me from the hill
overlooking Sheep Meadow so I ran to her
open arms and now I wish she was touching
this sarcen stone's silvery blue broach and its
sister with a rusty Saturn ring round its middle
alongside others who form a circle steaming
after a recent storm followed a Fall heat-wave
so warm air penetrates my skin as I lean
against these almost casual figures who lay

about unprotected without signs saying
"do not touch" they invite hugs and kisses
as they charmingly conjure grandma's
ghost and the words she whispered
about worshiping ancestors in the wilderness
when she comforted me as a child resembling
the great mother's surprising figure inside
the granite archways of Chartres' ruby
green violet and blue pouring through the arcs
of windows as light falls into the darkness
then pauses on the edge of a rose garden
by the back door overlooking wheat fields
that whirl with Prospect Park and Avebury plain
in my mind as dampness brushes my feet
and slivers of sunlight warm my whole body
as I cleave to the rough siding of these gentle
grey-blue giants in their speckled glory
trickling down each silvery crevice of sleep
where the secret-self hibernates below
the cloud banks till earth turns to Spring
delighting grandma on the park bench
as she waited for the sun bending over
the roof-tops of Brooklyn to touch her
face that rubbed mine in benediction

STONEHENGE

After dark dissolves, the sun splits and runs
through the stones' shadowy crevices.
Heat in my fingertips. Pale grey lichen.

Smudgy hieroglyphs. Summer's fiery pleasures
dissolve. Smatterings of frost. A chain fence
keeps us apart. I cling to the humming

light as Eros' arrow stings should
your words sear my flesh. I've hidden
your letters. We keep circling the past.

"Friends for life" sounds trite. Not so.
Does desire die? Is love seasonal?
Should we celebrate, or hold a funeral?

The sky is heavy with rain. Fear may freeze
these tiny shoots of hope. Kind words
defrost disappointment. We avoid saying

anything about the future. My body's unruly
imagination or serene meditations-- unpredictable
as this climate. It takes so little love to ignite

the threads cocooning my soul. Golden
feathered Hermes stands at the crossroads.
You've faded from sight. As a girl I enjoyed

competition in basketball, feared it in love,
running away when I found the boy I loved
with someone else. I run before the storm

into the underground tunnel back to the car-park.
Halloween ghosts flew from the New York subway
near Holy Cross Cemetery where my father's

buried. I never visit Brooklyn. Thick fogs
blanket the California coast in June
and July. Outside my window I see winter

storms brewing on the Pacific's edge. Huge
stones dot the brown hills of summer.
Our November green resembles your Salisbury Plain

on the island of my distant relatives, the Celts,
whose name I hid as a child, afraid of being
called an "outsider," my Mom being "non-Catholic."

Ethnicity in Brooklyn united and divided us.
We mingled on subways and buses,
in Flatbush Avenue stores. Rarely marrying

across ethnic lines-- Irish, Jewish, Afro-American,
German, Italian, English, Chinese, Puerto Rican.
You left your country for England.

Maybe our ancestors mated? The sun reaches
across the Atlantic then travels America
to reach this shore. You find the first light.

I miss our being in touch. Often I recall
the warmth you gave when I hid
in darkness. The electricity of your voice.

COLERIDGE NEAR GRASMERE

That house I loved with its vista across
the lake and below the sloping lawn a pier
waiting for us to sail. You arrived by foot,
having hiked fifteen miles. Such a far away
look in your eyes. I knew no one ought ever
to try and domesticate you. Your hands were
moving feverishly as you spoke of Schiller,
Kant and others you loved as we walked
through the dahlias and at lunch, drinking
red wine, your eyes gleamed with foreign
ports, exotic princesses, derelict spells
on the sea's surface, not a breeze stirred
and I couldn't get enough of you. Too soon
you were gone. Residue of your footprints
on the muddy path leading to the gate
where we said goodbye. Then in the distance
you turned and waved just before crossing
the hill heading home to your wife in Keswick.

RUSKIN'S VENICE

Sail boats skim the lake under a cloudy sky.
The wind picks up a hiker's "Hello."

After years of separation, finally
they're together. Hesitant, standing close

in the crowd, she fears offending those
who love them. Suddenly they're again

separated. "Not now. Maybe later."
He sought her bliss in paintings, travel

and literature. Why not an afternoon
in Venice when the air warms his skin

and the terra cotta walls overlooking
the lagoon glow with hope

till the sky turns turquoise
in the evening just above the yellow

window of the Ducal Palace. If only
beauty were always at hand

and not at a distance. Seeing her was
like seeing the streets of Venice

shimmering with a golden dampness
in all her details of lace and colored masks,

winged lions, domes, black boats and windows
unfurling pastel flags. Photos were painfully

incomplete. Memory played tricks on him.
Wasn't she walking on the opposite shore?

Her presence lingered by the edge
of all his dreams. They sailed into storms

of "No" "No." At night he reached for
his pen and paper as if his hands were on fire.

RUSKIN'S HOME, THE LAKE DISTRICT

Standing in your room with its windows
forming a cupola, looking out over Lake Coniston
I sense your nearness for the first time.
The fine beech window seat you carved

octagonally round these granite archways
you found in Italy. The light of an October
afternoon crosses your desk and touches
your forehead, though I can't see your eyes.

They are hidden and reserved,
as those Avebury stones set secretly
in earth. You are here and not here.
Your spirit stays and escapes this house

you built with its sweeping vista
over the lake where your emotions sailed--
those foolish, futile, romantic notions
so foreign to sensible visitors who scorned

your vain hope that she might eventually come.
But we do persist, don't we, no matter what
the circumstances, even as those stones
our ancestors placed on that plateau

to conjure the sun with such wide and tall
wishes to outstay the dark winter,
to attract among the stars one that might
scan the plains and see this all

too human hope-- as words on the page
seek a symmetry with such elements,
hidden and waiting for warmth and light,
as you did for her, hoping she'd come.

DURHAM CATHEDRAL

Autumn savoring the day's semi-dark
shifting aura. Candles refigured

every morning. Latin phrases fill
the sanctuary. Gabriel's arrival

in the cloister. You page a gold-leaf
Book of Hours. Please don't

disappear again Mercury, Cupid,
Artemis, Diana. Shoot your arrows.

My soul's waiting. Rain saturates
the soil. Steamy flagstones.

Your spirit haunts these aisles.
Rye bread, heady wine, prophecies.

October's blazing maples. Spring is
far away. I fly back to California

tomorrow. Rough serge clothed
my twenties. My monastic leanings

you laughingly ignored. If we spent
more time together you might

have listened. Offering incense,
petitions, contrition. Please receive

my thanksgiving. God help us all.
My son loves this church housing

Bede and Cuthbert. His first night
here he rubbed the gold letters

set in black marble. I caused both
my sons' suffering. Their love drew

me home. At the back of the church
the AIDS quilt is spread across

the granite floor.   I am reminded
of the many young San Franciscans

who have died of this virus.
Candles flare by Our Lady of Refuge.

TURNER AT THE TATE

Intense blue and pale yellow roam
these rooms I entered an hour ago,

after my first breathtaking experience
of your luminous castle over a Scottish lake

and misty promontory conjured
in San Jose, California

as dinner guests politely ask
"How was your trip?" while I drift

towards these dark blue canvases
streaked by Neapolitan orange,

Venetian gold flags over your shoulder.
Conversation lags, I fail to express

the tiny green pleasures
that splash a northern shore

or how Salisbury's spire still haunts
my thoughts as if I am actually "there."

Misty oaks, a brooding storm, inky
borders, distant hills, moody sunsets.

Pasta, wine and poached pears.
My guests press political subjects,

while somber violet lingers,
flashing red dominates,

charcoal hesitations, gold infusions,
passion and pure abstraction,

reliable villages mixing white with blue
above yellow straw fields,

black storms pressing grey uncertainty,
slight pink mornings,

then those flickering emotional
side-paths marked by scattered pebbles.

Finally your shadowy illusions
criss-crossing earth,

immaterial air caressing
sea and land throughout those last

brilliant yellow green years
when everything appeared singing--

foliage, clouds, morning, night,
cliff sides, waves, inmost fever,

perhaps your whole history
coalescing in serene unconcealed light.

VII

Death happens, love happens, and all human
life is compact of accident and chance. If one
loves what is frail and mortal, if one loves and
holds on . . must not one's love become changed?
There is only one absolute imperative, the
imperative to love . . .

> \- Iris Murdoch

. . . it is only by first trying to restore the past
that one comes to discover one's future path.

> \- W. H. Auden

BERKELEY AT LAST

An hour north of San Jose
the Golden Gate towers through fog.
I'm heading for a San Rafael Jungian,

recommended by a friend, having
learned too late how multitudinous
charm can conceal unwanted harm.

Promises made, soon enough broken.
At SFO I was berated for not trusting.
I've failed to follow ordinary warnings,

Drive slowly. Be cautious. Alcatraz
looms on the right. Visionary San
Francisco in my rear-view mirror.

Bicyclists speed on the western side,
tourists stroll the east. My mid-life
span. My falling from grace. Is

pardon possible? Who will absolve me?
Sausalito's white and blue ships.
Angel Island's misty history.

Dr. Litwiller's witty wisdom.
Sweet transference. The Richmond
Bridge brings me back to Berkeley,

Carol's garden. Callas singing
"Norma" in every room. Carrot soup,
seeded bread, artichoke salad.

A Chardonnay toast. Bees cling
to salvia buds. We stroll through
Live Oak Park. "You'll know nobility

of soul when you see it." She mends
broken stems (and damaged psyches),
saves seeds, propagates seedlings.

She hands me lavender cuttings
for my San Jose garden. "Be patient."
Waving goodbye, she blows kisses.

Treasure Island gleams by the Bay
Bridge. White foam splashing prows.
I-80's packed. Roses perfume my car.

PHOTOGRAPHY

Imogen Cunningham said she gave up
believing in complete self-forgetfulness,
instead settling for a sympathetic impression
of one person on another, the photographer's attempt

to merge. How Atget experienced Saint Cloud in 1910--
huge chestnut trees hugged the entrance road at dawn,
clouds pressing on white water, sun-shafts
calmed in a circular basin. This more than

satisfactory peculiarly hazed brown vision . . .
unrepeatable, never again captured in the way
such curiosity mediates desire
through the lens of intimate contrasts--

framing a tree's evocative nature,
personalizing a landscape in concentrated focus,
lighting and shading a subject, then the click
that yields or withholds surprises,

clothing and unclothing an illusion,
leading to your words, "Life is short."--
meaning "maybe" to my overtures,
though you add, "But I'm fond of you."

And my "Yes, and I of you" shaping
the implications in your silence.
We leaned forward as a fountain does,
or a gardenia about to bloom,

a stairway curved in on a shadowed invitation
suddenly withdrawn, "Bye now, have a good trip."
A river unable to define its future,
an alleyway refusing disclosure.

If I possessed Atget's grace, might we
have stayed close? No, I was kept carefully
as an observer. My body's camera,
poised and afraid, wanted never to forget,

though in time we all do. I photographed
your face in my heart's contractions,
framing your room with ivy and cyclamens
on the window-sill. This sufficed, until

years later in a darkened drawer I find
the negatives. Brooding your absence,
I lift the delicate paper to lamp-light,
seeing the lines where your presence developed.

AFTER A SEVEN YEAR DROUGHT

You say your depression made you withdraw.
I'm moved and surprised by your self-disclosure.

Such honesty regarding moods is rare in our extroverted
culture where men are pressured not to show emotion.

Not much has happened since I last wrote, except
finally after a seven year drought an abundant storm.

The pollen is incredible; everyone seems to be
sneezing. Irises buried for years in our yard

are popping up all over. Outside the kitchen door
a gardenia's scent. A profusion of fuchsia,

larks and hummingbirds. Daffodils are multiplying
after the rain's return. But first the messenger

of hope-- those pink almond buds under a blue
San Jose sky. The bees are pressing gold.

Wisteria thickens on Mission Santa Clara's adobe
wall, though, as you say, all this beauty

can't guarantee happiness. Still, I hope this
yellow lantana keeps till you open my letter.

NEW CAMALDOLI HERMITAGE, BIG SUR

High on a ridge in the Los Padres National Forest
this hovering eight-sided room where men
are singing *Hosanna* and *Alleluia.*
as hawks call in air currents sent by
the Pacific blue as a woman is rubbing
black cinders off a particularly
gnarled redwood near a stone circle
she has arranged over the years,
having shaped the stream last winter,
when she wore tall boots and rough gloves,
lifting the large stones to coax
the rushing water through crevices,
past pebbles and boulders, round sharp
granite helping the river to sing
under her window, bubbling up and leaping
near two deer whose black moist noses
glow in the sun during these terribly dry
September days when the hills are a tinder-box
of brown bushes set afire by last week's
lightning strike, now showering flakes

of ash amid billows of false fog, causing
local evacuations and the wish for the rainy
season to splash through the triangle
of redwoods bridging the ravine
as she hears the monks chanting above
in their holiest room for the rain's return.

THE ALMOND TREE, SAN JOSE, CALIFORNIA

for Joseph, Edwin and Peter

You built a cabin on top a ridge
in the Santa Cruz mountains offering a sweeping
view of Monterey Bay clear across to Carmel.
We poured the concrete foundation with friends.
Our young sons played hide and seek in the redwoods.

Outside the kitchen window a northern sky
kept turning on its wheel of stars.
October's warm ocean, January's severe storms.
Our road is washed away. We sell the cabin.
Does this mean we will give up dreaming?

The following February we're at home
in San Jose, California, startled by
the almond tree in our backyard,
countless clusters of pink-white buds,
pinwheels falling over Mrs. Ferrara's fence.

Hermes, our golden cat, eyes a hummingbird.
Lavender penstemon dusts the bee's belly.
We put away winter clothes, sip a lemon tea
with honey, call each other those pet-names
we invented when we first came west.

SANCTUARY

She finds the bronze phoenix feeding her young.
A red-tailed hawk flies to her shoulder. Rain drips
slowly on the green slate roof into the courtyard.
Cracks in an ancient stone well. Aloe stars along
the wall. Candles flickering on the ledge. "Once
more out of darkness deliverance." Silence ignites
the syllables she says over and over. Love's a flame
on her tongue. She dances to flute music circling
the sanctuary. Golden incense burners. Smoke
rising round her waist. God's messenger smiles.
His tattered wings held close. Thunder and lightning.
Cymbals and hand-clapping. Sunlit wing-tips.
Colors swirl in the stained glass windows telling
the story of her life. The divine child rests in her arms.
No grief or hope goes unattended. Every hour
of every day the door near her alcove stays open . . .

FANTASIA, GOLDEN GATE PARK, SAN FRANCISCO

for Joseph

He stands by the green reeds and wild irises
of Stowe Lake. On the left a waterfall tumbles
over grey boulders near paddle boats and a red
Japanese pagoda. A white heron across the lake.
Joggers run past the eucalyptus grove. Yellow-green
bamboo waves behind the Buddha's head
near the black and gold footbridge where his dark
smile illumines the lotus opening its heart.
She rubs the moist carpet of bluish moss.
His lips brush hers under the white and pink
plum blossoms as they lean against a redwood.
A brown sheen of winter pine needles
blankets the path. Their arms round each other's
waist. Overhead the discs of quaking aspens.

The Breastplate of St. Patrick

hrist with me,

Christ before me,

Christ behind me,

Christ within me,

Christ beneath me,

Christ above me,

Christ on my right,

Christ on my left,

Christ when I lie down,

Christ when I sit down,

Christ when I arise,

Christ in the heart of every man
who thinks of me,

Christ in the mouth of everyone
who speaks of me,

Christ in every eye that sees me,

Christ in every ear who hears me.

Then the herb garden where Francis
faces a pond filled with milky-white lilies.
His fingers open to a host of black and yellow
chickadees who sip the liquid streaming
through the circle of ecstasy in his palms.
A sign says-- "Feel free to touch and taste."
They pick basil, rosemary and sage, reminding
them of the North Beach Italian restaurant
where they ate lunch. He offers her a bunch
of tiny purple buds and she smells his hand,
where the sprigs lay, recognizing the lavender
that mingles with a familiar feline scent,
golden Hermes, whom he pets every morning.

NATURAL BRIDGES, SANTA CRUZ, CALIFORNIA

in memory of James Merrill

This earthen bridge I loved years ago--
gradually left land. In my twenties I swam
these icy waters. No bottled message
saying you shall return.

America ends here at this very coast.
The sun slowly slips where water meets sky.
Light and darkness commingling.
Do spirits haunt this western rim?

Tide pools where I walked with my young sons.
Sea soaked mossy channels brush these
gorgeous anemones that we mustn't touch.
Do the dead wear disguises--

animal, bird, fish, flower . . .
a thick kelp forest sluicing alongside
the sea's pulsating humor,
wavy lines flip over

and over, suddenly surf-crests
act up, recede, turn quiet, hiss.
Your thoughts and desires,
everything near and dear,

then the scented eucalyptus grove,
where the monarchs return for nectar--
wings brushing a particular lover
quickly before the incoming fog.

Fierce waves pierce misty mornings.
A sea-bird's orange webbed toes hug the broken
bridge. Pelicans glide home by sunset. Surfers
dream the big one will arrive tomorrow.

Your witty tidal phrases, clever gyrations
through cocoons of memory and habit.
Butterflies leap in my psyche,
should your body fall away.

WISTERIA OUT WEST

On Long Island's western shore
the Sound sometimes subdues the Atlantic.

Funny, at the time I didn't get it,
thinking each green swell

splashing over the mossy edge of grey stone
as an envoy of the unconscious,

not realizing what I was setting
in motion, romantic seascapes without

a clear picture of the players--
myself, God, Nature, a friend or lover?

Hunches, silences, perhaps a pattern--
as I walked alone round the pond's

waist-high rushes, where a crane went
into hiding. Something was about-to-happen,

though there was no clear warning.
The horizon drew a stunning sunset

across the fluent sea, then suddenly
things darkened. I lost perspective.

The birches wore stark white coverings.
Geraniums and lantana were without flower.

I needed the reassuring wisteria that cast
its discs fifteen feet across the yard

reminding me how the psyche can split open
in "letting go" saying "no" making "yes"

a future happening as it was . . waiting
at the beginning, here at home, out west.

FLYING HOME FROM HOBOKEN, NEW JERSEY

You're wearing a green shirt, your silvery hair
framed by Manhattan across the harbor as you lean
on the railing. Dark churning waters of the Hudson.
As kids we rode the train with Mom, Dad and John
along the river to Bear Mountain. Hoboken is a hub
for subways, ferries and the bus we take through
the Jersey meadows, past factories, high risers,
sports arenas, shopping malls and the green foothills
of Rockland County's Ramapo range with maples, birches,
pines, oaks and elms rising in hills till we reach your town
of Sloatsburg ringed by a baseball field, swimming pool,
forests, lakes like Sebago and Tiaroti in Harriman Park
by your back door where we sip wine before dinner
as your three girls listen to our stories about Brooklyn

when Loretta and I played baseball, tag
and basketball with you and your friends
in Holy Cross School yard. On Sunday your son
Tim marries Maureen at Manhattan College
where Joe studied engineering before entering
Maryknoll. The wedding reception is along
Long Island Sound's Davenport Landing,
where Joe's Dad sank his money into a country club
and Joe worked tables as a seminarian in the summer.
Next week we'll take the train to Hoboken,
then the Hudson tubes to the World Trade Center.
We'll hug goodbye outside your office at Madison
Square Garden across the street from Father Henry's
apartment ministry to those "outside" the church.
I'll catch the shuttle to Grand Central where I used to
ride the train through Harlem, up the Hudson
to Maryknoll and years later across to Connecticut.
The Carey bus stops on Park Avenue, a few blocks
from the Maryknoll House at 121 East 39th Street
where I worked as a secretary after high school,
south of Sun Chemical on Lexington and 48th Street
where I first found an office job after leaving the convent.
I often called Joe from the red public phone box
at the corner of 46th Street. The bus to JFK bypasses
Brooklyn via the Holland Tunnel into Queens. A hazy
Williamsburg Building in the distance. The plane banks
above Riis Park beach where Dad taught us swimming
a half hour from Flatbush Avenue and our rented rooms
on Lott Street and East 26th Street, close to our alma mater,
Brooklyn College, John's Midwood High, your Erasmus Hall,
grandma and grandpa's beloved Prospect Park and the cherry
trees we ran under in the Botanical gardens where we met
grandma on summer afternoons near Grand Army Plaza's
Public Library where Dad and I went on Saturday mornings
on the same bus I rode to Saint Joseph's High School
near the Brooklyn Bridge and Myrtle Avenue El train
to the East New York orphanage I visited on Tuesdays
where the little ones called me "sister." Then flying
west, the lights of the George Washington Bridge . . .

MENDOCINO HEADLANDS, WHALE WATCHING

moist spider webs and thistle-down criss-cross my legs

as the morning breeze rises off this cliff overlooking the Pacific

yet it rarely happens except in religion that we call

such phenomena miraculous forgetting ordinary immortality

exists in amber rocks moon tides sea anemones and abalone

while we humans insist our lives matter more than these

superfluous thrills and tumbling waves trickling back

and forth gold-veined and salty with serpentine tongues reigning

in the sun's momentary warmth into these ancient pools

carving an open-ended roughly caved subtly smooth rendezvous

of islands cliffs and headlands as we scan the Pacific sighting

the whales slow motioning 5 miles per hour Arctic bound from Baja

6 or 7 clusters 20 in less than 30 minutes unveiling white

barnacled black shoulders rising and falling in roll on roll

after another pregnant March these mothers calves and male

guardians overseeing all the white foam rhythmic spouting

as they swerve through violet green kelp bed forests

tails brushing a Far Eastern blue kindred spirits to our Bed

& Breakfast's misty purple iris folds falling in bright pollen showers by the cypress while dreamy under a comforter

we slip in and out this coast's savory green hills suggesting

ambrosial embraces work well for humans as in California's

Baja basin reenacting their species' intelligent playful tumbling

towards instinctual bliss such mammal manoeuvres undiminished

by interference they wink as they leap the whales moving on ...

TO LOSE
(Inverness, California / Luxembourg Gardens, Paris)

> "To lose
> But to lose truly
> To give way to discovery"
> -- Apollinaire

To lose you in a sea of strangers
    and find you again
        in those distilled moments,
        without regret

In the dream the man and woman
    on the foot-bridge see
        the large flowered jelly-fish breathing
        in the stream disappear
        and reappear

Now she believes at one time he too
    found this beach

It is the day after they met
    and now she knows nothing
        about where he is . . .

Still the green shade exists
    half way round the world
        where Neptune smiles
            in the shade of plane trees
                and moss entangles his toes

The lilies rise in their pale lavender petals
    once more to the surface of Spring

Desire is a burning coal
    in the heart of the rose

The magnolia opens
    her yellow eyes and sees
        beyond the forest

She cups her hands and calls
    to the moon and stars
        who travel endlessly

I stop along the path
    where the willow spreads
        a canopy of silvery wands
            over the young couple
                who promise to love
                    each other forever

The season of summer remains
    in the orange and yellow dahlias

A child is sending a ship in the circular pond

It is now that I recall your voice

AN AFTERWORD

In every life there are the inevitable experiences of loss-- whether of a beloved person, an animal, a time, a place, a profession, a sense of the sacred, whatever . . . . Sometimes, when we lose what is dear to us, it is as if we have lost something of our very self. Yet, Proust believed, and I am a devoted reader of his work, that the past is buried in layers of our sensual memory. We need only recover what is waiting within. By seeking in my past as to "why" certain things happened, I was led further back into my childhood and further yet into my grandmother's history to the world of my family's beginnings. In writing about "what was" I relived those experiences in the now of "what is." The literary critic Louis Martz calls this kind of writing "meditative poetry"-- a way of setting the stage visually for particular persons, places, scenes or events to interact and become presences who inform the poem.

By reimagining my grandmother's Scotland, my childhood in Flatbush, Brooklyn, the years as a Maryknoll Sister overlooking the Hudson River Valley or at the Novitiate in Topsfield, Massachusetts, to the early days of my marriage and mid-life challenges on the east and west coasts, including vacations in England, Scotland and France- I was once again "there." No one "voice" of the self comes through in these poems, rather the "voices" of different times, places and versions of myself and of those I have loved. We hear of "a garden of lost paradise"-- maybe moments of our "lost worlds" are available at any time, as Proust would have us believe, if we travel back and forth between times past and present. I wish you, dear reader, the joy of the journey and the comfort of companions who travel along and welcome you home.

-- Carolyn Grassi